Spinning
in the Old Way

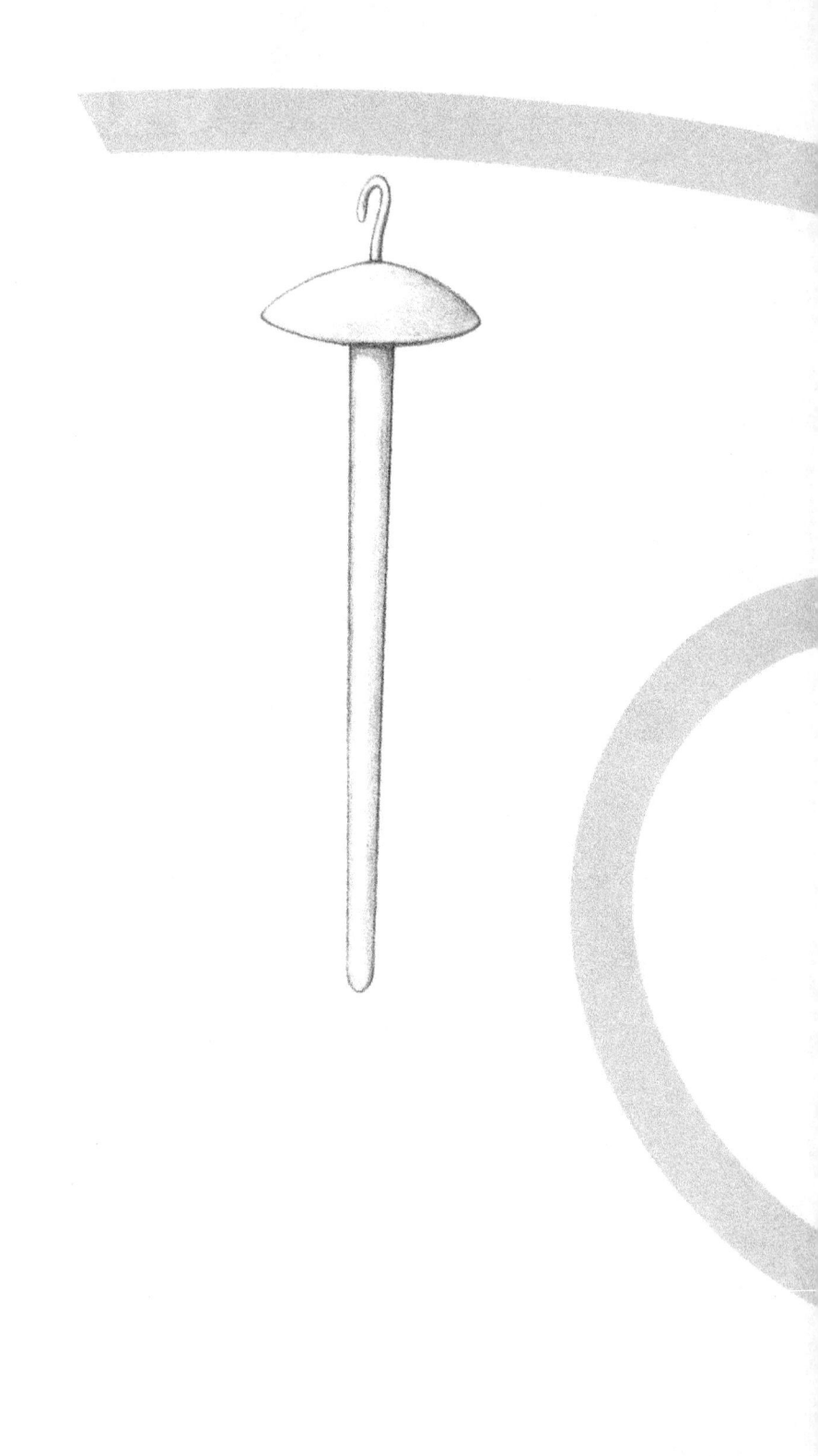

Spinning in the Old Way

*How (and why)
to make your own yarn
with a high-whorl handspindle*

by **Priscilla A. Gibson-Roberts**
with illustrations by **Susan Strawn**
based on drawings by Priscilla A. Gibson-Roberts

ECHO POINT BOOKS & MEDIA, LLC
Brattleboro, Vermont

Published by Echo Point Books & Media
Brattleboro, Vermont
www.EchoPointBooks.com

All rights reserved.
Neither this work nor any portions thereof may be reproduced, stored in a retrieval system, or transmitted in any capacity without written permission from the publisher.

Copyright © 2006, 2025 by Priscilla A. Gibson-Roberts

Spinning in the Old Way
ISBN: 978-1-63561-959-1 (casebound)
         978-1-63561-983-6 (paperback)

Editing and interior design by Debra Robinson
Illustrations by Susan Strawn
Indexing by Katie Banks / Eagle-Eye Indexing

Cover design by Kaitlyn Whitaker
Cover art: Spindle art by Susan Strawn; background by Kiwihug; courtesy of Unsplash

The text is set in Worstveld Hand (Graham Meade;Typotheticals). Additional type includes Worstveld Sling and Worstveld Sting (Graham Meade; Typotheticals); Mazurka (Nick Curtis; Nick's Fonts); Poetica Chancery and Swash Capitals (Robert Slimbach; Adobe); and Altemus Arabesques, Pinwheels, and Spirals (Robert Altemus; Altemus Creative). The mix is lightly seasoned with Rustic Sage Ornaments (Sage Reynolds; T.26), P22 Woodtype Extras Two (P22), Directions (Monotype), Bembo Semibold (Stanley Morison, Francesco Griffo, Giovanni Tagliente, Aldus Manutius; Adobe), and LTC Goudy Oldstyle (Frederic W. Goudy; Lanston Type Company).

Books by Priscilla A. Gibson-Roberts

Spinning in the Old Way: How (and Why) to Make Your Own Yarn with a High-Whorl Handspindle (Nomad Press, 2006)

Knitting in the Old Way: Designs and Techniques from Ethnic Sweaters (Nomad Press, 2004; with Deborah Robson)

Simple Socks, Plain and Fancy (Nomad Press, 2001, 2004)

High Whorling: A Spinner's Guide to an Old-World Skill (Nomad Press, 1998)

Ethnic Socks and Stockings: A Compendium of Eastern Design and Technique (XRX, 1995)

Salish Indian Sweaters: A Pacific Northwest Tradition (Dos Tejedoras, 1989)

Knitting in the Old Way (Interweave Press, 1985)

Contents

Acknowledgments		8
Preface		9
Introduction		11
1	In praise of the high-whorl spindle	
	A top-notch tool for every spinner	20
2	Getting started	
	You CAN make your own yarn	28
3	Spindles and supplementary tools	
	The right equipment makes it easy	44
4	Fibers and fiber preparation	
	Choose good-quality materials and prepare them well	62
5	Spinning technique	
	Discover methods that will work for YOU	90
6	Singles, plies, and cables	
	Many different yarns, from simple to complex	128
7	Finishing your yarn	
	Better than store-bought	158
Afterword		169
Selected suppliers		170
Suggested reading		173
Index		174

Acknowledgments

To acknowledge all who have contributed to my work in spinning with the high-whorl spindle would be overwhelming, so I will limit myself to those directly involved in the day-to-day reality of this book. First, my husband, Jack, for understanding my need to write this book and his willingness to become a partner in my work as well as my life. And, as always, my indispensable friends: Nelda Davis for always being there, no matter what; Noel Thurner for her enthusiasm and support in my every endeavor; Anna Zilboorg and David Oliver for their support on the first edition, without which this book would not have come into being. And also I honor those who laid the foundation many years ago: Grace Crowfoot, with *Methods of Handspinning in Egypt and the Sudan,* and Bette Hochberg, with *Handspindles.*

Preface

*It really is **this easy** to make your **own yarn**.*

Before you begin, here are a few basic definitions and a brief introduction to the high-whorl handspindle, the topic of this book and one of the most treasured discoveries of my life.

It really is this easy to make your own yarn.

Spinning

Loose fibers become yarn because of *twist,* which holds them together. A bunch of loose fibers will just fall apart if you pull on their ends. But as soon as you twist them together, they become yarn and can't be pulled apart as easily. (You can break yarn, but it won't simply drift apart . . . unless it hasn't been twisted enough.)

Spindles

The spindle is a tool that lets you quickly and efficiently put twist into loose fibers, turning them

into yarn. It is also a temporary storage device for your newly spun yarn, which is wound around its shaft until you have enough to skein off or wind into a ball.

There are many types of handspindles.

High-whorling is what I call spinning with a high-whorl handspindle, a spindle with the circular weight at the top of the spindle's shaft. The high-whorl versions of the handspindle are so distinctive that they deserve their own verb for the action of using them to make yarn by hand.

This is the type of spindle that changed my life. I can do without my spinning wheels. I cannot do without a high-whorl spindle.

What you need to begin spinning with a high-whorl handspindle

- A spindle
- Some unspun fiber
- A length of sportweight wool yarn

See pages 29–30 for my recommendations of what to get.

That's all!

Introduction

How I discovered what I'm about to share with you, and what it means in my life

I ambled down a long, circuitous route to find my niche in craft. It has taken more years than I care to recall. But the journey was rewarding—so many good memories as I sought what I refer to as "my destiny." I found that destiny: high-whorling is my calling. I follow it wherever it takes me.

I began my involvement in spinning, as did many in the early revival days of the 1960s and 1970s, with little guidance and with makeshift tools, often of my own devising, all with few redeeming features except that they served as a starting place. The few commercially available tools of the time were rarely available to me. I was primarily a nomadic spinner and knitter, moving through the boondocks of the arid West. The tools and supplies of the era were advertised in weaving journals, to which I had little access.

In retrospect, this was a minor inconvenience. The commercially available tools at the time were clunkers, rarely better than my homemade efforts. Few contemporary spinning wheels were being made. I had no interest in acquiring an antique. An old wheel would have required too much restoration before it could be a functional piece of equipment, and then I would have had to pack it up and cart it hither and yon, wherever my geologist husband's work took us next. I struggled along as best as I could, using my improvised tools.

And then I came upon the spinning wheel of my dreams. It was a small, sturdy, handcrafted upright wheel, lovingly referred to as "Little Thumper." It was perfect for a person with limited space and high mobility. I said goodbye to handspindles with little regret.

Thus began my odyssey of finding my "self" within my dual craft of spinning and knitting. Textiles and ethnic clothing, both contemporary and historical, had long been my passion. I slipped naturally into the study of ethnic sweaters, re-creating the old classics, always using my own handspun yarns.

The result was my first book: the original edition of *Knitting in the Old Way*. It was a survey, and by definition could not reach any depths of information about the styles of garments that it gathered together. So I delved deeply into the part of my

Introduction

survey that I found most intriguing: the Cowichan sweater. This garment has traditionally been made exclusively of handspun yarns, spun in the early years on spindles and then on the Indian-head adaptation of the spinning wheel. The result of this further work was a second book, called *Salish Indian Sweaters* (an unfortunate title, because it incorporates the tribal name instead of crediting the Cowichan band, within which the distinctive sweaters originated—a concern that I am addressing in that book's revised edition).

I wanted to get to the bottom of things....

By this time, I knew that it was not sweaters I wanted to document, even when they were made exclusively of handspun yarn. I wanted to find the roots of the craft, to get to the bottom of things. I needed to go farther back in time to find my soul.

Instead, I found soles: I studied historical socks. In the beginning, all the old socks that I could find to examine came from western and northern Europe. Too few had been made of handspun yarns. I was not satisfied. Then a pair of Eastern socks came into my hands: they were exquisite handspun, handknitted works of art. This was it: my soul truly soared, for here was the beginning, the roots of

> ### Western and Eastern sock traditions
> My studies led me to two distinctly different sock traditions, which I call European and Eastern. The Western socks came from the western and northern parts of Europe. The Eastern socks came from eastern Europe, the Middle East, and Central Asia.

Spinning in the Old Way

My first experience with high-whorling was not merely satisfactory—it was exhilarating!

No more fiddling and fumbling.

Just straightforward,

simple spinning.

knitting. And these roots were dependent on spinning. Yes, many of today's Eastern socks are made of commercially spun yarns, but the old ones were not!

In studying the socks that I recorded in my third book, *Ethnic Socks and Stockings,* I discovered the use and value of the high-whorl handspindle.

This simple tool never was replaced by spinning-wheel technology through much of Scandinavia and the North Sea islands, as well as in parts of Eastern Europe, the Middle East, and Central Asia. In the north countries, the spindle remained in use in conjunction with the spinning wheel. The spindle provided much needed mobility, so spinning could continue regardless of the spinner's location. In the eastern realms, the high-whorl spindle was and is the tool of choice, partly because nomadic ways survived in many areas. However, even in settled communities the spinning wheel either was never introduced or, if it was, never gained popularity.

My first experience with high-whorling was not merely satisfactory—it was exhilarating! At last,

Introduction

this was a spindle I could relate to: no more fiddling and fumbling, just straightforward, simple spinning.

That first high-whorl spindle was not finely crafted. It consisted of a plywood whorl, a dowel, and huge hook, but it was well-balanced and inexpensive.

With the acquisition of a finely crafted reproduction spindle from Iceland, I was off and running. There seemed to be little learning involved. Yes, I studied everything I could lay my hands on about the high-whorl spindle and the various cultures that spawned these tools. Most of the information I found consisted of drawings and photographs, often in publications written in languages I did not know. Luckily, I seemed to understand what to do to fill in the gaps. Instinct? Or written in my genes, as some say?

To me, my connection with this tool seems even more profound than that. In part because I lived the life of a modern nomad for so many years, moving from water project to water project all over the drylands of the Western states, my attraction to the spindle, the spinning, and the knitting felt much deeper than can be rationally described. In ways that I cannot explain, I feel that in some far-distant past I traversed the steppes of Central Asia, high-whorling and knitting the hours away, working as the demands of daily living permitted—producing socks out of need, creating works of art out of desire. Not an easy life, stripped of all but necessities and facing the realities of a harsh environment, but

a life that stayed close to the land, a life that remained at one with the seasons and surroundings.

Yes, high-whorling seems more a matter of recall than learning. This feeling brings peace to my soul.

What is so wonderful about making yarn with a high-whorl spindle?

By now you might wonder what is so wonderful about high-whorling.

Simplicity

Simplicity comes to mind first. All my "necessaries" can fit in a small bag: spindle, *nostepinne* (the Norwegian word for a wooden tool used for winding a ball of yarn), niddy-noddy (skein winder), and occasionally what I refer to as plying rods (in my case, a set of old wooden knitting needles), along with some prepared fibers.

Mobility

Then mobility. I spin anywhere, whenever I have a moment, whether I am alone or in a crowd. This is something to consider even for those who are devoted to spinning-wheel technology: high-whorling can significantly increase your yarn production by letting you use odd bits of time, both at home and abroad.

Versatility

Next, versatility. I can make any kind of yarn—woolen or worsted, high-twist or low-twist, fine or bulky—and always with precise control. I have read that some of the most meticulous weavers in Scandinavia would never dream of spinning their warp by any means other than on a handspindle. In

Introduction

High-whorling seems more a matter of recall than learning.

This feeling brings peace to my soul.

their opinion, a spinning wheel was fine for making the weft, where minor inconsistencies would not threaten the weaving's sound structure!

High quality

And, for those on a limited budget, high-whorling is very economical. Top-of-the-line handcrafted tools can be obtained for a small investment. And if money is still a concern, homemade tools are an option for those who have the skills to make them (or have a willing and skillful friend).

Economy

Now that so many high-quality, commercially prepared fibers are available, you need nothing more than a spindle, a nostepinne, and a niddy-noddy. If you prefer to begin with raw fleece, as I do, you can add a pair of hand carders and/or simple hand-held combs.

High-whorling is fast, thus negating the most common complaint about making yarn with a handspindle. A well-balanced high-whorl spindle is a real production tool, regardless of the type of yarn you want to make. With this spindle, you can reach the speed of an average spinning wheel. At the same time, you can minutely control the flow

Speed

The techniques presented here represent my way of high-whorling—not "the" way of high-whorling.

Every spinner needs to take what is applicable and adapt it to an individual working style.

Easy on the spinner

of fiber and twist, the two elements that determine the ultimate quality of your yarn.

Last, but of utmost importance to me: high-whorling does not tax the body. With mounting physical limitations, I seek out activities that I can do in comfort. With high-whorling, I can sit, stand, or move around. Because I am able to maintain proper body alignment, there is no strain on any part of my body. All this without suffering any loss of productivity!

Yes, high-whorling is for me. I do still have my two spinning wheels, but I think more and more frequently about passing them along to another spinner. Any object that sits idle, taking up space while acquiring layers of dust, seems impractical when my goal is a simple, somewhat austere life

Introduction

and when an alternative tool is available that does not require me to make any compromises.

I need to emphasize that the material in this book is based on research but the details I present have been obtained through practical experience. Historical resources for the information I sought were scarce. My interests lay primarily in the nonliterate cultures; much of the printed information that I found had been based on assumptions. So when I could not find historical evidence—for example, about using the nostepinne for plying—I improvised, as any true peasant would do.

The techniques presented here offer one set of methods for accomplishing the tasks involved in making high-quality yarn with a high-whorl spindle. This is my way of high-whorling—not "the" way of high-whorling. Every spinner needs to take what is applicable and adapt it to an individual working style.

Spinning is a hand craft: its rules are not carved in stone.

HANDCRAFTSMANSHIP... JUSTIFIES ITSELF AT ANY TIME AS AN ULTIMATE EXPRESSION OF THE SPIRIT.

Soetsu Yanagi, *The Unknown Craftsman*

In praise of the high-whorl spindle
A top-notch tool for every spinner

There are many types of handspindles, but most fall into one of two categories, based on the position of the whorl on the shaft: the high-whorl and the low-whorl handspindles. On this topic I am very opinionated: the high-whorl is superior.

The low-whorl spindle is better-known among Western handspinners because it has come down through our heritage from Colonial America and Western Europe. The high-whorl spindle developed in the Middle East and Central Asia. One reason that people in America and Europe did not use the high-whorl handspindle was that they simply did not have information about the design and use of this spindle style. Because it was not part of our history and culture, the high-whorl spindle was not available to us until a relatively short time ago.

We can safely say that the high-whorl handspindle has been in use for at least forty centuries (yes, that's four thousand years—and this tool was

Spinning in the Old Way

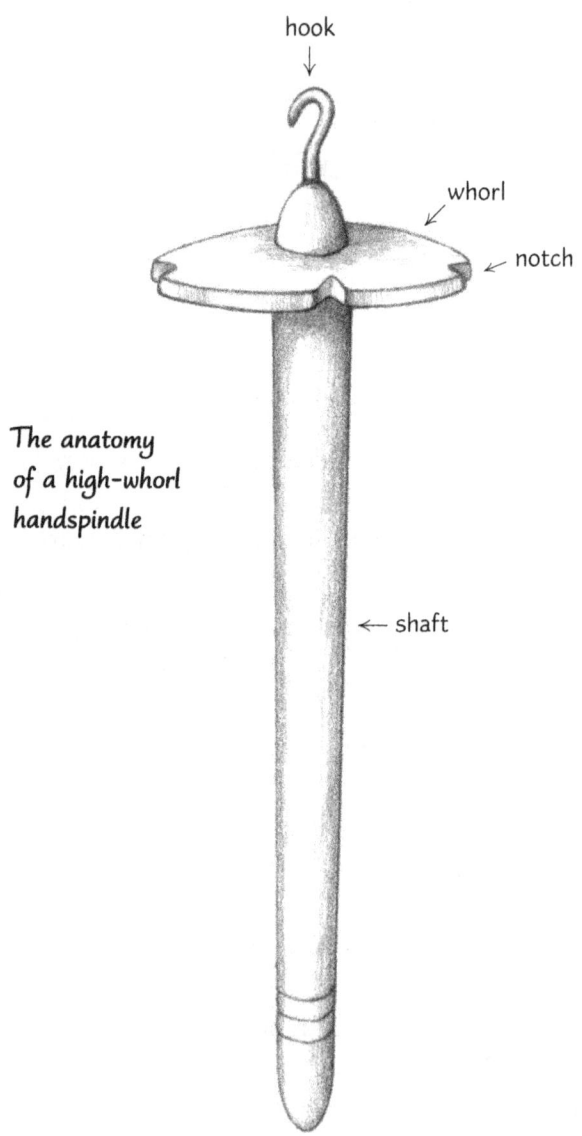

The anatomy of a high-whorl handspindle

In praise of the high-whorl spindle

all but ignored during the spinning "revival" of the 1960s and 1970s).[1] Egyptians still call the whorl placed at the top of the shaft *ras el maghzal,* "the head of the spindle."[2] Although first used for linen, this type of spindle is now more commonly used for wool. It can be used with any spinnable fiber.

Only in archaeological studies of Egyptian tombs do we find significant general information about the high-whorl handspindle. The friezes of some tombs clearly depict people using this tool to turn flax into fine yarn, destined to be woven into the world-famous linens of ancient Egypt.

The use of the high-whorl handspindle was not limited to Egypt. It has been the preferred spinning tool for diverse ethnic groups, from Africa (among the Bedouins and Sudanese) north to the steppes of Central Asia and east to Eastern Europe. The high-whorl spindle was also common in Scandinavia and the North Sea islands. Although many Scandinavian and North Sea people embraced spinning-wheel technology, the wheel never completely replaced the high-whorl spindle.

1 Grace Crowfoot, *Methods of Handspinning in Egypt and the Sudan* (Halifax, England: County Borough of Halifax, 1931), page 30.
2 Bette Hochberg, *Spin, Span, Spun* (Santa Cruz, California: Bette and Bernard Hochberg, 1977).

Spinning in the Old Way

Advantages of the high-whorl spindle

In recent years I have become aware of a groundswell of interest in the ease and efficiency of the high-whorl spindle among both beginning and skilled handspinners. So I offer here my opinionated comparison bewteen high-whorl and low-whorl handspindles.

Whorl position

The most obvious difference between low- and high-whorl spindles is the position of the whorl on the shaft, although closer inspection will reveal many other advantages to the high-whorl construction.

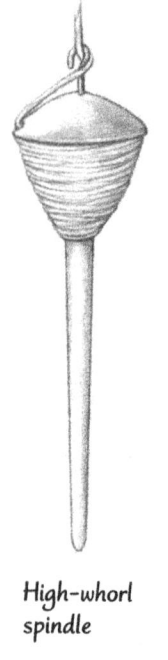

High-whorl spindle

Low-whorl spindle

The location of the whorl determines the motions the spinner uses to rotate the spindle. With a high-whorl design, you rotate the spindle by rolling the lower section of the shaft on your thigh in one fluid motion. This technique produces great speed with little effort. To rotate the low-whorl spindle, you twirl the upper end of the shaft with your fingers. I find this both much slower and more demanding on my hands.

In praise of the high-whorl spindle

Basic low-whorl handspindle types

1 Low-whorl spindle with hook
The yarn spirals up the shaft, barber-pole–style, and threads through a hook.

2 Low-whorl spindle with half-hitch
The yarn wraps around the lower end of the shaft, then comes to the tip of the upper shaft and is secured to the shaft with a half-hitch.

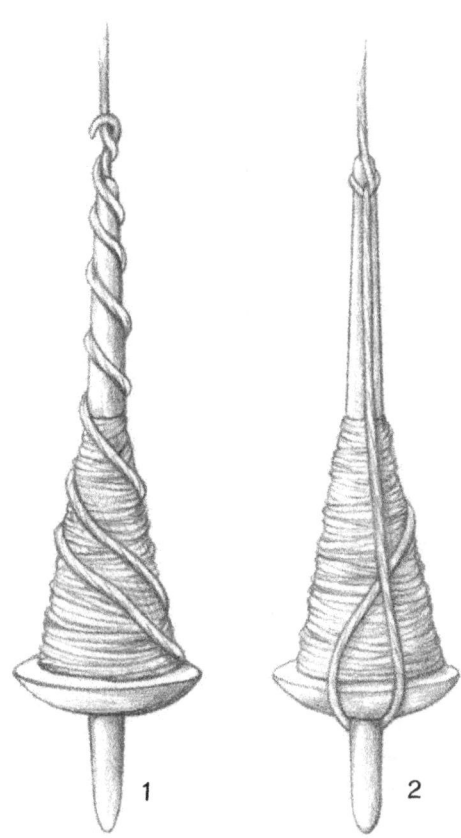

Means of securing the yarn at the spindle's top

On both spindles, you need to be able to secure the already-spun yarn to the spindle's top while you are spinning. Otherwise the completed yarn, wrapped around the spindle for storage, will unwrap when you rotate the spindle—and the spindle will immediately plummet to the floor.

Low-whorl spindles can have any of several alternatives for securing the yarn. The top of its

Spinning in the Old Way

Classic high-whorl handspindle

The yarn catches in the notch and passes through the hook.

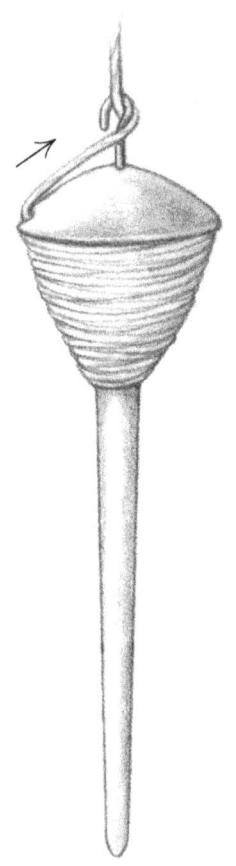

shaft (located at the opposite end from the whorl) may be smooth, notched, or fitted with a hook.

On many low-whorl spindles, before you begin to spin you wrap the yarn under the whorl and secure it around the lower portion of the shaft, then take it to the top and attach it a second time with a half-hitch. I call this the *low-whorl with shaft hitch*. For me, this double-attachment is a fum-

In praise of the high-whorl spindle

bling procedure that must be done each time you spin a length of yarn.

On a low-whorl spindle that has a hook at the top of the shaft, you can't just take the yarn right to the hook and start spinning. Again, the spindle will drop to the ground unless the yarn is well secured. You must either wrap the yarn under the whorl, as on the previous model, or must spiral the yarn up to the top, barber-pole—style, to develop tension in the yarn before you slip it through the hook. After you spin a length, you must reverse these processes before you can wind the yarn onto the shaft for storage. I call this the *low-whorl with hook* design.

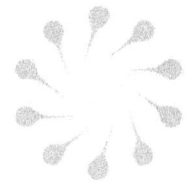

Most high-whorl spindles have a hook at the top of the shaft (the same end where the whorl is located).

On what I call the *classic high-whorl spindle,* the yarn is tucked into a notch on the whorl, then goes up and through the hook. Spinning continues immediately—a straightforward process. Unhooking to wind a new length of yarn onto the shaft for storage is equally simple.

Handwork, because it has nature behind it, has a way of fostering the good life.

Soetsu Yanagi, *The Unknown Craftsman*

» 2 «

Getting started
You CAN make your own yarn

This chapter is devoted to taking up the high-whorl handspindle for the first time, whether you have never spun before or you have experience in spinning with a low-whorl spindle or a wheel. Don't be concerned with the fine points of tools and techniques at this point. I'll help you refine your approach in the next chapters.

Supplies

You will need three things to start spinning:

- A good, basic, high-whorl *spindle* that weighs between 2 and 2.6 ounces (between 60 and 75 grams).
- Some carded wool *roving*. If possible, get a heathered blend—you'll find it easier to see the twist in your yarn. I recommend one of the longer wools, and am especially fond of wool from Romney sheep

1. Spindle
2. Roving (wool)
3. Length of commercial yarn

for beginners, although a number of other breeds produce similarly suitable fiber. Six ounces (170 grams) will be plenty to start with.

- A length of *commercially spun yarn*. I suggest between 10 and 12 yards (9 and 11 meters) of two-ply wool sportweight yarn.

There are many places to obtain these materials. Your yarn shop may have spindles and roving. If not, see pages 170–172 for some ways to find them. The yarn can come from your stash, or from a friend's.

Which hand does what? Standing or sitting?

Spinning is an ambidextrous craft. Both hands contribute equally. I will go through this process referring to your *dominant hand* and your *assisting hand*. Sooner or later, you may discover that it's fun and useful to be able to perform each part of the process with either hand. The only "rule" is to do what is comfortable for you.

The high-whorl spindle can be used from either a standing or a seated position. You will probably find it easiest to go through the first, practice steps while standing, as shown in the illustrations. When you begin to work with roving, I will suggest that you initially sit. As you continue, choose the position that's most convenient.

Getting started

Ideas you will refer to frequently

Suspended or supported?

There are two basic ways to use a high-whorl spindle: (1) with the spindle hanging suspended from the yarn that you are spinning or (2) with the spindle supported, or resting on something (usually your leg).

You will meet both of these techniques in this first chapter. You will use the suspended method when you stand up and practice with a length of commercial yarn, and you will use the supported method when you sit down and begin to draft fiber.

Which direction do I turn the spindle?

A handspindle rotates in two possible directions. You can turn the spindle in either direction, although once you have started spinning in one direction you need to continue in that direction until you wind the yarn off the spindle. Otherwise you'll simply untwist what you've twisted.

Depending on which way you turn the spindle, the resulting yarn is known as either S-twist or Z-twist yarn. The angle of the twist in the yarn will match the middle portion of the letter S or the letter Z.

How do I tell which way is clockwise?

By looking down at the top of the whorl!

If the top of the whorl is turning in a clockwise direction, you will be spinning Z-twist yarn. If the top of the whorl is turning in a counterclockwise direction, you will be spinning S-twist yarn.

Z twist (left), shown with a single strand, and S twist (right), shown with a plied yarn.

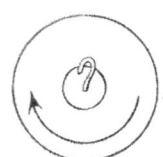

Clockwise

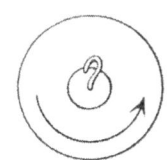

Counterclockwise

Spinning in the Old Way

Practicing with a length of yarn

To familiarize yourself with the way the high-whorl spindle works, begin by practicing with the length of yarn instead of starting with roving. This will let you experiment with the movements without being worried about dropping the spindle. If you are new to spinning, you will also begin to understand how twist behaves.

Attaching the starter yarn to the spindle

Begin by attaching the starter yarn, a length of two-ply commercial sportweight wool yarn, to the shaft of the spindle.

1. Secure the yarn to the shaft. ~ Fold the length of yarn in half; then secure it to the shaft by drawing the two ends through the fold.

　　Holding the shaft in your dominant hand, throw the yarn ends across your opposite shoulder, out of the way, as shown in the small drawing to the left.

2. Then thread the doubled strand of yarn through the notch and hook. ~ With your assisting hand, grasp the yarn about 24 inches (60 cm) from the hook. Take the yarn up through a notch, then around the hook with one clockwise turn.

Getting started

Setting up the spindle

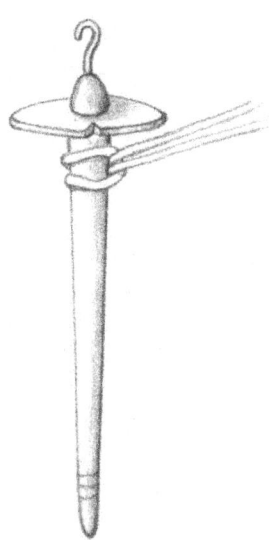
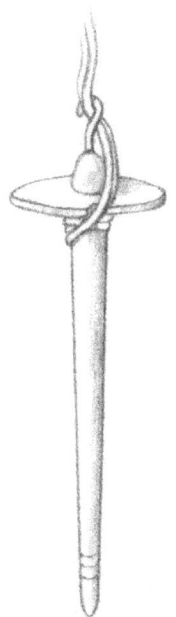

Step 1:
Securing the yarn to the shaft

Fold the strand in half and draw the two ends through the fold.

Step 2:
Threading the yarn through the hook

Take both strands up through the notch in the whorl and around the hook.

Taking the yarn around the hook

Either direction will work, although there are traditions for using clockwise or counterclockwise turns that will be explained. As long as you choose one direction and stick with it, you will be fine.

Spinning in the Old Way

Twisting in the first direction

3. You are now ready to experience the elegant way in which rotation is imparted to the spindle: by rolling it along your thigh. With your dominant hand, roll the shaft UP your thigh.

4. Then release the spindle, letting it hang suspended on the yarn while it turns. As the spindle rotates, twist will travel up the yarn toward your assisting hand.

Step 3:
Beginning to twist
Begin to insert twist by rolling the shaft of the spindle up your thigh.

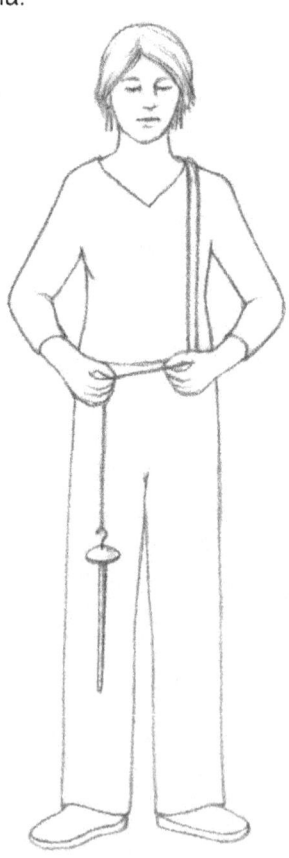

Step 4:
Suspending the spindle
Let the spindle hang from the yarn and turn. Twist will enter the yarn as the spindle rotates.

Getting started

5. Grasp the bottom of the shaft and unwind the yarn from the hook.

6. With the shaft in your dominant hand, turn the whorl away from your body. Rotate the shaft clockwise to wind the yarn onto the spindle. This will be the same direction that you wound the yarn to attach it originally and that the spindle turned when you were spinning. Keep the yarn that you are winding on the part of the shaft close to the whorl.

Go back to step 2 (threading the yarn through the hook) and repeat the process again and again until you reach the end of the yarn.

**Steps 5 and 6:
Winding the yarn onto the spindle**

With its whorl facing away from you, turn the spindle's shaft in your hand and wind the yarn onto the shaft.

Spinning in the Old Way

Twisting in the other direction

Now wind the yarn off the spindle and go through this process again, except this time roll the shaft DOWN your thigh and wind the yarn onto the hook and onto the shaft in a counterclockwise direction.

You'll notice that you need to remove the twist put in during your first session before twist can enter the yarn in the opposite direction. Experiment with this principle for a short while, not for the whole length of the yarn. Right now I just want you to understand both directions of twist and how only one direction can be used at a time.

"Drafting"

There's one more aspect of spinning that I would like you to practice with the yarn before you begin working with roving. This is the way your hands will coordinate when you do what is called *drafting* when you are working with the unspun fibers.

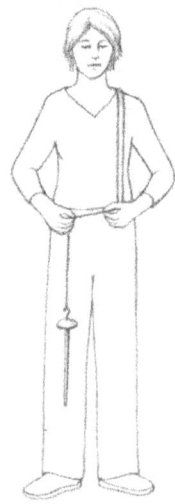

In drafting, you gently tease enough fibers out of the fiber supply to make the size of yarn that you want to spin.

Go back to rolling the spindle UP your thigh, but this time add another step in the process. This happens in step 4, when the spindle is suspended and rotating. The two strands of yarn are being twisted together.

This time:

Getting started

1. With your dominant hand (the one that rolls the spindle), pinch the strands of yarn together about two feet above the hook while they are twisted (see the small drawing on the opposite page).

2. With your other hand, gently pinch the yarn together just above the first hand. Then slide your upper hand along the strands of untwisted yarn for another 24 inches (60 cm) or so. This sliding movement of the hands away from each other is how your hands will coordinate when you *draft* the fibers (also called *drawing out*).

   There's one more action in this sequence.

3. After the yarn below your first hand is twisted, release the pinch of your first hand's fingers and allow the twist to travel up the strands until it reaches the second hand.

   Now it's time to wind the yarn onto the spindle.

Practicing with the yarn

Try these sets of movements a few times. End your last practice run with the commercial yarn by rolling the spindle UP your thigh.

Spinning with roving

Now you are ready to make your own yarn from the carded roving. I recommend sitting down to learn this part. You will be able to control the spindle better while you are getting the idea of how to draft the fiber. Continue to roll the spindle UP your thigh.

Leave some of the commercial yarn you used for practice wound onto the shaft. You will want to have between 4 and 6 inches (10 and 15 cm) of the yarn extending above the hook. You will attach the fibers from the roving to this yarn to get yourself started. This starter yarn is called a leader. Tie the two ends of this doubled yarn together with an overhand knot.

The roving will be in a long, loose strand. Pull off a piece about 36 inches (91 cm) long. (Don't cut the fiber: cut ends make fiber hard to spin.) Divide this strand into four lengthwise strips. Work gently, separating the roving in half and then separating each of those sections in half again. Set three of these pieces aside. You can wind each extra piece loosely around your fingers to make a little bird's-nest shape to keep it orderly until you are ready for it.

Drape one strip of the roving over your shoulder, in the same way that you previously arranged the commercial yarn. Gently draw out some fibers from the end of this strip: loosen them to make a fringe that is not as thick as the section from which they are being drawn. Lay this fringe of fibers through

Getting started

the loop formed by the knot of the leader. Use your second hand to hold the fibers and the leader next to each other. Now you are ready to go through the spinning process, step by step.

This time, support the spindle on your thigh instead of suspending it. You will roll with your dominant (first) hand along the thigh on the same side. Roll the shaft UP your thigh to insert twist into the fibers..

Drafting

1. Draft out a short length of fiber, elongating about 2 to 3 inches (5 to 7.5 cm) of roving. Feather out the fibers from the end of the strip.

2. Roll the shaft UP the thigh several times to build twist in the drawn-out fiber.

3. Let the handspindle lie on your thigh. Grasp the twisted fiber with the fingers of your first hand. Pinch the fibers also with your second hand. As you start this process, your second hand will pinch right next to your first hand. In the next step, your two hands will move apart.

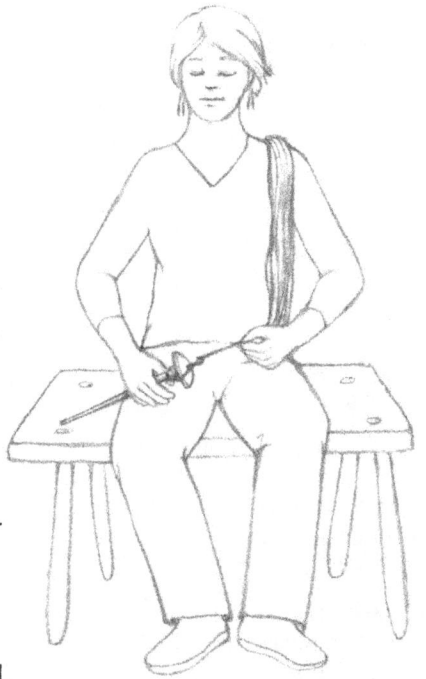

Steps 1, 2, and 3: Drafting the fiber

Draft out a short length of fiber, then roll the spindle shaft up your thigh several times to build up twist.

Spinning in the Old Way

**Steps 4 and 5:
Drafting, and controlling the twist**

Control the flow of the twist into the fiber with your dominant hand, using the pressure of your thumb and forefinger against each other with the fiber in between.

Use your other hand to draft out more fiber. Repeat until all the stored twist has been used to form yarn from the fiber.

4. As you did before, draw out the fibers with your second hand, preparing a length of about 2 to 3 inches (5 to 7.5 cm). Your first hand continues to pinch. It keeps the twist from traveling up toward your second hand and the undrafted fibers.

Controlling the twist

5. Release the twist from the first hand as shown in the drawing, freeing the twist to travel up the drafted fibers to the second hand.

Repeat steps 4 and 5 until you have created a comfortable length of yarn—somewhere between 12 and 24 inches' worth (30 and 60 cm).

Getting started

Wind your yarn onto the spindle shaft in the same way that you wound your practice yarn.

Then draft and spin a new section of yarn.

Joining more fiber

When you come to the end of the first roving strip, leave a small section unspun. Feather it out. Also feather out the beginning end of the new strip. Overlap these two feathered sections and spin them together.

Use the same technique to rejoin the roving if you break off in the middle of a strip while you are spinning: feather both ends, overlap them, and continue the process.

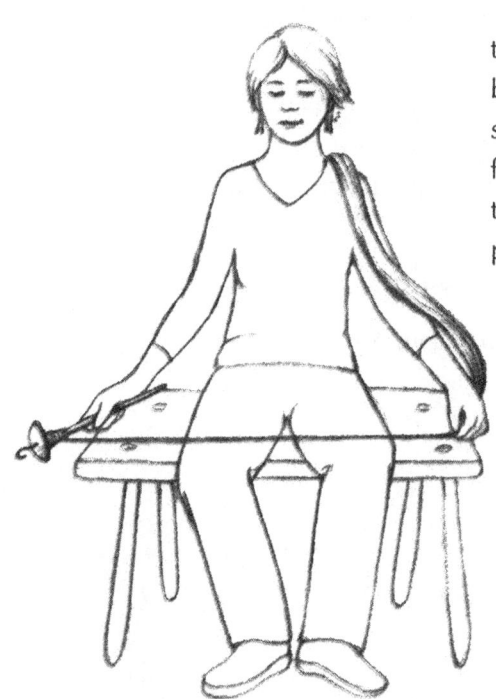

Winding the yarn onto the spindle
Use the same technique that you used when you were practicing with the yarn (page 35).

Smoother and faster, while seated

Once you are comfortable with this phase of learning, you are ready to put it all together in a continuous process.

Still working from a seated position, draw out a short length of fibers. Roll the shaft with your first hand as before. Immediately after you roll the spindle, move your first hand up to control the flow of the twist at the same time that you draw the fibers out of the roving with your second hand. You will soon be able to draft more than once with each roll of the shaft.

Work in this manner, winding the finished yarn onto the spindle shaft when you need to get it out of your way, until you are comfortable with continuous drafting.

Smoother and faster, standing up

Now stand up and work in the same manner with the spindle suspended.

You now have yarn. You have conquered the basics and are ready to go on to the fine points of selecting equipment and fibers as well as the technical aspects of handspinning.

Getting started

That's it! You know how to spin yarn!

Everything else you learn here will make you a more efficient spinner and will give you more control over the yarn you make. But the "hard" part is already behind you!

Not

  so

     difficult,

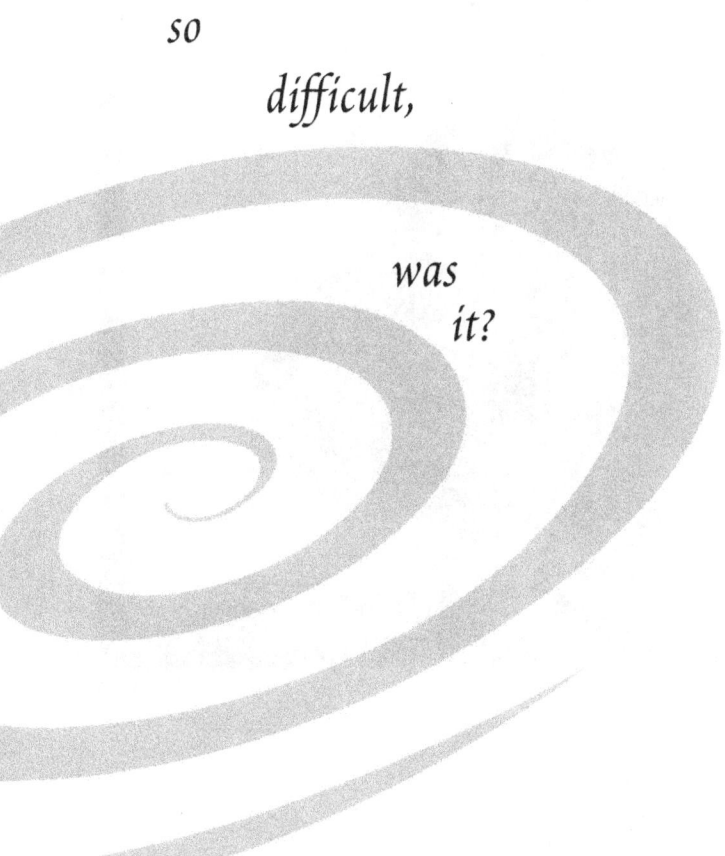

        was
         it?

LOVELY THINGS ARE ALMOST ALWAYS SIMPLY MADE.

Soetsu Yanagi, *The Unknown Craftsman*

… 3 …

Spindles and supplementary tools
The right equipment makes it easy

The first consideration in choosing a handspindle is weight. The weight determines what type of yarn you can spin comfortably on any given spindle.

This does not mean that you must have a dozen or more spindles to spin a full range of yarn. For most spinners one spindle is sufficient, as each of us tends to work most often within a fairly narrow range of yarn types. With two spindles, you can cover a wide range of yarns, while with three you should be able to make any yarn you can imagine, from very fine to very bulky.

I need to stress that the perfect spindle does not exist. For spinners learning their skill, I recommend a good-quality basic tool in the 60–75-gram range (2.1–2.6 ounces). Once you have some experience, you can select additional spindles that fit your style and preferences. Spindles are sufficiently inexpensive that you can try a variety until you find one, or more, that you love.

Spinning in the Old Way

Unless you are a collector, do not buy for looks alone. For the real spinner, the high-whorl spindle is a tool. The fact that it can also be beautiful is a bonus! (See pages 170–172 for some sources for spindles. New suppliers appear frequently, so it makes sense to learn to evaluate the spindle in front of you.)

Talking about sizes of yarns

While the terms *sportweight, worsted,* and *bulky* are enough to differentiate commercial yarn weights, when you make your own yarn you need to learn additional ways of describing its size. When you have a practical way to tell exactly where the yarn you are making fits into the big picture, you will be able to spin a yarn that fits the purpose you have in mind.

Fortunately, a low-tech, easy-to-use measurement system exists.

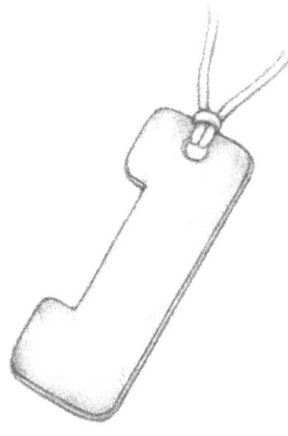

This is a yarn gauge. It has been handcrafted from wood and equipped with a cord, so it can hang around your neck.

I prefer a cylindrical yarn gauge, made by cutting an inch-long notch in a dowel, to a flat, rectangular gauge. The cylindrical form supports more even tension. With a cylindrical gauge, you can rotate the tool to draw the yarn around it, instead of winding on by hand.

What is most important is that you use a gauge!

Spindles and supplementary tools

Wraps per inch (w.p.i.) is the number of time a yarn can be wrapped around an object within a one-inch span. Wrap loosely enough that the yarn retains its normal loft. Nestle the wraps next to each other so they fully cover the object they are being wound around without being crowded.

In this example, the yarn measures 7 w.p.i. and its diameter is 1/7 inch.

Wraps per inch

You can directly determine a yarn's size by wrapping the yarn around a ruler, a small yarn gauge, or even a pencil, and counting the number of wraps contained within an inch. This is called, sensibly enough, *wraps per inch* (w.p.i.). (If you are working metrically, you can use any convenient base measurement as long as you use it consistently. The equivalent of wraps per inch is the number of wraps in 2.5 cm.)

The diameter of the yarn, in inches, is the reciprocal of this number. In other words, if your yarn measures 10 wraps per inch, then the yarn's diameter is 1/10 inch.

Two-ply yarn types and the spindle weights to produce them

Yarn type	Wraps per inch (or 2.5 cm)	Spindle weight	
very bulky	11 or fewer	75 grams	2 2/3 ounces
bulky	11	50 grams	1 3/4 ounces
knitting worsted	12	50–75 grams	1 3/4 – 2 2/3 ounces
DK	13	50–75 grams	1 3/4 – 2 2/3 ounces
sportweight	14	25–50 grams	7/8 – 1 3/4 ounces
Shetland	15	25–50 grams	7/8 – 1 3/4 ounces
fingering weight and laceweight	16, 18, or more	10 grams	1/3 ounce

Plying is the spinning-together of two or more strands to make a finished yarn. A two-ply yarn combines two single strands.

Plying can be done to make a thicker yarn, to add strength, or as a design technique.

Which spindle for which size of yarn?

Use the charts on these pages to determine which weight of spindle to use when you want to make a specific size of yarn. The charts apply specifically to the production of two-ply yarns, which are the workhorses of the handspun world, although they can also guide you to the right tool for making singles (one-strand yarns) or more complex yarns, with many plies, cabled constructions, and the like.

Spindles and supplementary tools

Spindles are individual. Their weights probably will not exactly match what you see in these charts.

However, you clearly won't want to use a ½-ounce spindle to make worsted-weight yarn!

Spindle weights and the two-ply yarn types for which they work best

Spindle weight		Spindle's versatility	Yarn type	Wraps per inch (or 2.5 cm)
75 grams	2⅔ ounces	Versatile for heavier yarns	very bulky	11 or fewer
			knitting worsted	12
			DK	13
50 grams	1¾ ounces	Most versatile weight, useful for all yarns except the very finest and the most bulky	bulky	11
			knitting worsted	12
			DK	13
			sportweight	14
			Shetland	15
25 grams	⅞ ounce	Lightweight yarns	sportweight	14
			Shetland	15
10 grams	⅓ ounce	Very fine yarns	fingering weight	16
			laceweight	18 or more

Recognizing a good high-whorl spindle

All high-whorl spindles are not created equal. There are a number of finely crafted spindles available, and there are also many that look elegant but are poorly designed. Therefore it is important for you to learn how to recognize quality.

The hook

We'll begin at the top, with the hook. Many people will try to convince you that a hook is a hook. Not so! A poor hook can make an otherwise good spindle nearly useless.

Why is the hook so important? With every length of yarn that you spin, you must guide the yarn onto and off of the hook. If this is not effortless, your spinning rhythm will be broken and your frustration will rise.

I like a high, elongated hook, in which the highest point in the upper curve is centered over the base of

Hook styles for high-whorl handspindles

Elongated hook.   Swan's-neck hook.   High-peaked hook.

Spindles and supplementary tools

the hook, where it attaches to the spindle top. My favorite hook is a handcrafted brass swan's-neck style, followed closely by a commercially produced stainless-steel hook from Scandinavia.

The high-peaked hook is another handcrafted style that can be good. This hook is bent at an angle, instead of being curved, and is usually found on smaller handspindles.

On some spindles, the hook can appear to have very little neck. Closer inspection reveals that the spindle's shaft itself serves as the neck of the hook. In this case, the tip of the shaft should be shaped so that there is a graceful join between the shaft and the curve of the hook, so you can smoothly slide the yarn into place when you wrap it onto the hook. If the neck rises vertically to a flat edge, the yarn may lodge at the corner of the hook rather than move up to its top; this will cause the spindle to wobble when it turns.

Cup hooks are among the least desirable hooks for spindles, because the yarn often comes to rest

Shaft serving as the neck of the hook: look for a graceful join.

Cup hook: a round hook with a vertical neck.

On a cup hook, the yarn tends to rest on the neck of the hook, instead of at the top of the curve.

Spinning in the Old Way

on the neck of the hook rather than at the top of its curve. A more suitable commercially available alternative is a fine-gauge ceiling hook, a very sturdy hook somewhat similar to the swan's-neck version that I like.

The whorl

Position of whorl on shaft

Next take a look at the whorl. The whorl's shape, size, and weight vary considerably with the materials used and the design of the tool. Because many handspindles are handmade, I cannot cover all possible variations. I can, however, suggest general characteristics to consider when you select your spindle.

The first is the *position of the whorl on the shaft*. In most cases the whorl is placed at the top of the shaft, although on some high-whorl spindles the whorl can be located as much as a quarter of the way down the shaft. Spindles with the whorl at the top tend to dance a bit when you first start to load them with yarn. They settle down after you have completed and wound on several lengths.

A whorl located farther down the shaft is more stable from the first turn of the spindle. In addition, you can rotate it either by turning it with your hand or by rolling it on your leg. On the other hand, a spindle with a down-shaft whorl cannot hold as much completed yarn as can a spindle with its whorl at the top. Ultimately, you will choose the spindle style that feels right to you; this will

Spindles and supplementary tools

Placement of the whorl on the shaft

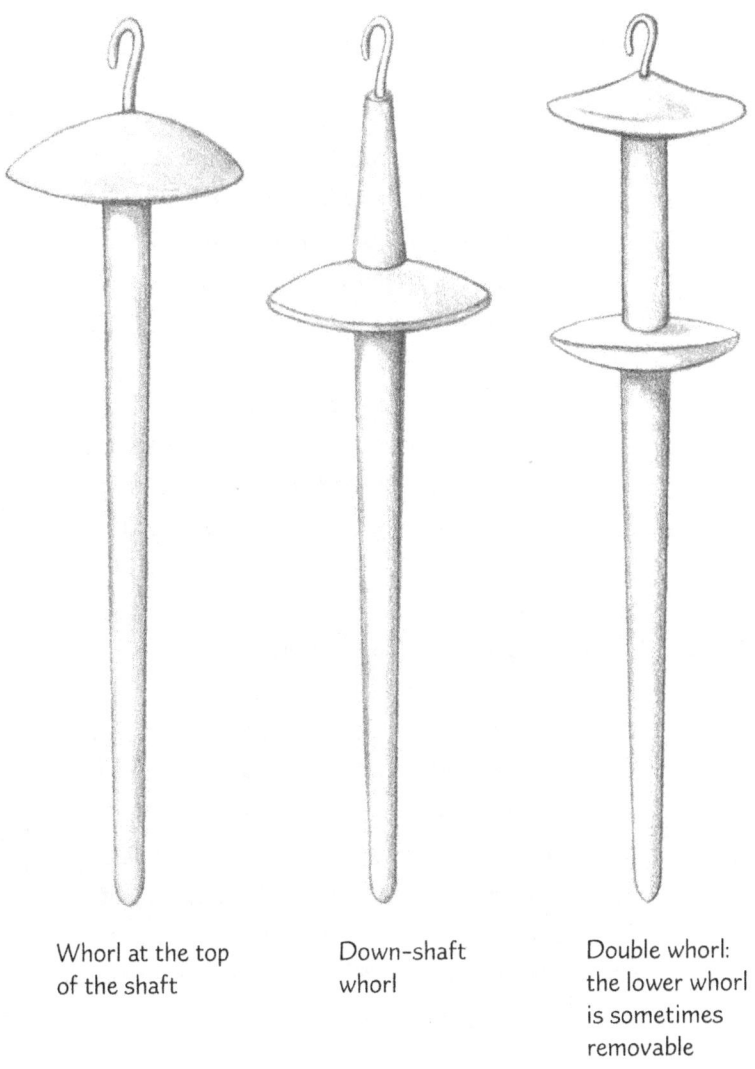

Whorl at the top of the shaft

Down-shaft whorl

Double whorl: the lower whorl is sometimes removable

Spinning in the Old Way

become the determining factor in your selection of whorl positions.

A whorl can be *permanently attached* or can be *removable*. Spindles with attached whorls are bulkier to store and are more prone to minor scrapes and bruises when carried around (though these signs of use can also produce a comforting handspindle patina). Spindles with removable whorls are easy to store, but as soon as yarn is wound on the shaft you lose this advantage. If you take the whorl off with the yarn in place, your neatly wound cop will become distorted.

Whorl attached or removable

Removable whorls can be secured in either of two ways: with a *friction fit* of whorl to shaft or by being *screwed onto a threaded shaft*.

Friction-fit whorls may slide onto the shaft either from the base up or from the top down. Each version has some disadvantages. Unless carefully fitted, a friction-fit whorl put on from the top can slip upward from the pressure of the yarn on the shaft. Similarly, one put on from the bottom up can slide downward quickly if the spindle is bumped at the base of its shaft.

In my opinion, removable whorls are most desirable when a single shaft is designed to be used with either of two whorls, one the primary whorl for spinning singles and the second a heavier whorl for plying.

Double-whorl spindle

You may also come across *double-whorl spindles*. One whorl (fixed) is at the top of the spindle and a second (removable) is partway down

Spindles and supplementary tools

the shaft. The lower whorl weights the spindle and steadies the rotation until the first few lengths of spun yarn have been wound on. After you have built up the first part of the cop, you can remove the lower whorl. This second whorl can also provide extra pull for spinning heavier yarns, greatly extending the range of yarn sizes possible. In addition, the second whorl can increase the spindle's weight to facilitate plying.

Cop is the name for the clump of spun yarn that has been wound onto the spindle shaft for storage. Cops can be wound in a variety of shapes, which I'll cover later.

The notches on the whorl

I think that notches on the whorl are imperative. Many beautiful spindles do not have them, because they would interfere with the aesthetic design of the whorl. As my high-whorl spindles are tools first and works of art second, I add notches if they are not provided by the maker. You don't want a tiny notch; you want one big enough to handle both singles and plied yarns.

The shape of the notches that can be used depends on the shape of the whorl. Drawings of the alternatives are on the next page.

Shapes of notches

Spindle whorls are commonly *flat* or *domed*.

On a domed whorl, a notch can be cut at an angle through the edge where the domed top surface meets the flat base.

On a flat whorl, a notch can be cut vertically through the side. There are several types of notch: the classic V notch often found on old spindles; a straight-edge vertical cut; and a semicircle. I much

Spinning in the Old Way

A domed whorl with a notch cut at an angle where the dome meets the base.

Placement of notches

prefer the semicircle notch because it secures yarns of a wide range of diameters and doesn't let them slip.

The *placement of the notches in relation to the hook opening* is also important. If there is only one notch, it can be located directly in front of or behind the opening of the hook. A notch behind the opening of the hook is preferable to one in front, because if the notch is in front the yarn may tend to catch in the corner of the hook. With two notches, they can be located on each side of the hook (my preference) or directly in front of and behind it. With three notches, the first should be directly in front of or behind the hook opening and

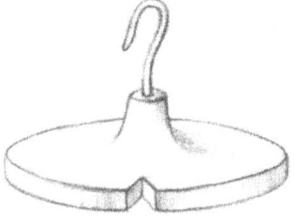

A classic V notch cut in a vertical edge.

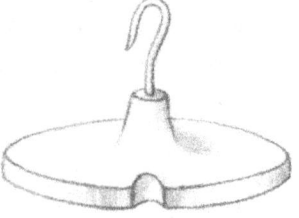

A semicircle cut in a vertical edge—my choice.

Spindles and supplementary tools

Placement of the notches in relation to the opening of the hook

1 One notch: placed directly in front of or behind the opening of the hook.

2 Two notches: on opposite sides of the hook, either in front of and behind the opening or (my preference) perpendicular to the opening of the hook.

3 Three notches, equally spaced around the whorl, with one directly in front of the hook opening.

4 Four notches, same concept as for three notches.

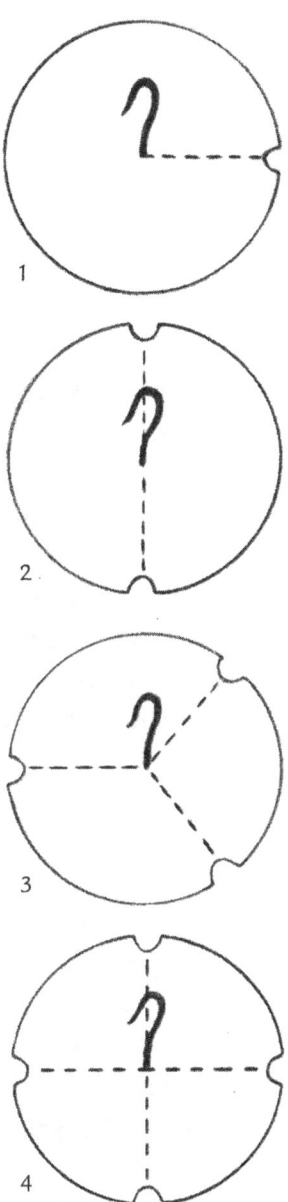

the other two should be evenly spaced around the circumference of the whorl.

The shaft

Although it may seem unimportant, the shaft can determine whether your spinning is pain or pleasure.

Shaft made from a dowel

First, beware of a shaft made from a *dowel*. This kind of spindle can be a good learning tool. However, dowels have a tendency to warp in time. When that happens, the spindle wobbles and becomes a frustration.

Shaft turned on a lathe

A shaft that has been *turned on a lathe* will be much more dependable over the long run. One disadvantage of the turned shaft is that most are so smoothly finished that the yarn will not pack densely around the shaft and the cop will tend to shift downward. Unless you wind on carefully, you can end up with a mushy cop that will be hard to work with.

Shaft shaped with a drawknife

A shaft *shaped with a drawknife* will have flattened areas that you may not be able to see, but that you can readily feel with your hand. These slight irregularities allow the yarn to grip the shaft, making it easier to wind on. In addition, the slight texture is less likely to slide when you roll the spindle on your thigh, so you can develop good rotational speed. The same effects can be obtained by cutting vertical grooves along an otherwise smooth shaft.

Tapered rather than straight

I like a tapered shaft rather than a straight one. With a tapered shaft, it is easy to slip the cop off the spindle's shaft and onto a plying rod (see page

Spindles and supplementary tools

61). Similarly, a shaft decorated with fancy turnings makes it hard to remove the cop by any means other than winding it off.

Finally, the shaft must be long enough to accommodate both the yarn and your hand. A small spindle can be rotated with your fingers alone, so its shaft does not have to be as long as the shaft on a heavier spindle. When you are spinning a thick yarn on a heavy spindle, you will need the full force of your hand. In general, the shaft on small spindle can be between 7 and 8½ inches (17.8 and 21.5 cm) long while the staff on a larger spindle should be between 12 and 15 inches (30.5 and 38 cm) long.

Length of shaft

Supplementary tools

When you are serious about high-whorling, you will want to consider adding a few more tools to your spinning bag. I will explain how to use these items later. For now, I will introduce you to the rest of the things you may want—in part so you will realize how compact your spinning equipment will be, and in part so you can begin to become familiar with the variety of tools and look for those that will become your favorites!

You will make good use of a *nostepinne* (ball-winding stick), a *niddy-noddy* (skein winder), and, occasionally, *plying rods* for making yarns with multiple plies. These tools are readily available, and most variations of them are serviceable.

1 **Nostepinne**
2 **Niddy-noddy**
3 **Plying rods**

Spinning in the Old Way

Nostepinne

A nostepinne is a wooden tool used to wind a center-pull ball of yarn. I recommend a spinner's nostepinne, which is smooth (with few decorative turnings), has a shallow groove for securing the yarn, and is steeply angled from base to top. You can ply directly from this type, whereas a deep groove can, on occasion, snag the singles when you use the nostepinne for plying. (Ball-winding with the nostepinne is described on pages 150 to 151, and plying with one is on pages 151 to 153.)

Noddy-noddy

A niddy-noddy has four arms and is used to wind skeins. The old standard size for niddy-noddies produces a 2-yard (1.8-m) skein and an overall length of about 18 inches (46 cm).

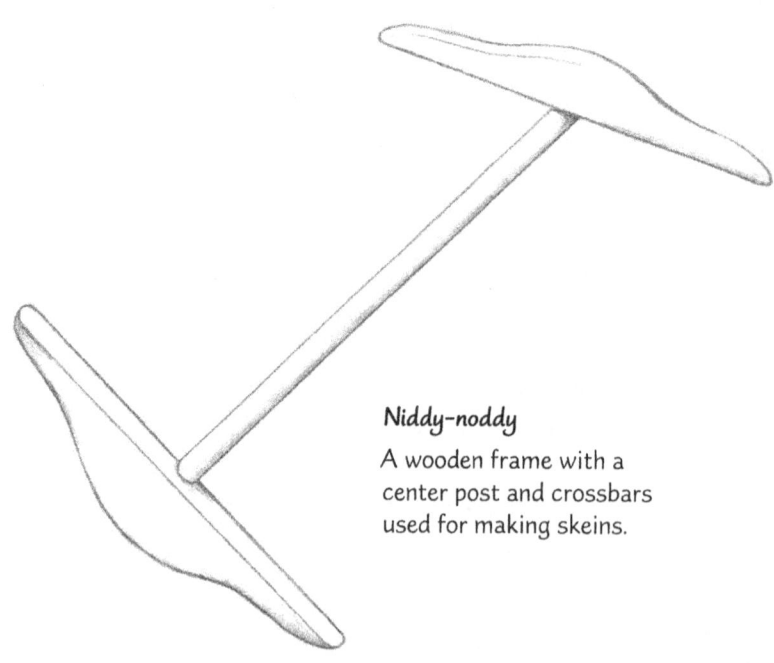

Niddy-noddy
A wooden frame with a center post and crossbars used for making skeins.

Spindles and supplementary tools

I suggest something smaller for ease in winding yarn off a handspindle. I much prefer a 1½-yard (1.4-m) niddy-noddy (one with an overall length of about 13½ inches [34 cm]). This size is easy to use when you are seated without stretching your arms into awkward positions. Removable crosspieces are a big plus, because they make the niddy-noddy much easier to carry around. Instructions for using a niddy-noddy are on pages 159 to 162.)

Plying sticks can be large wooden knitting needles, or you can make them from pointed dowels. (I explain how to use them on pages 153 to 154.)

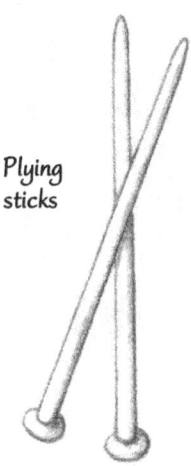

Plying sticks

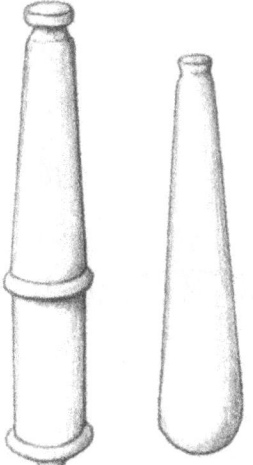

Two types of nostepinne

A knitter's nostepinne (left) and a spinner's nostepinne (right). The yarn feeds smoothly off the spinner's version, so you can ply directly from it.

Some nostepinnes now have a vertical notch across the top instead of a groove around the tip. I now prefer this style. Catch the end of the yarn in the notch and its end will be held in place by the yarn being wound into a ball.

Work done with the heart and hand is ultimately worship of life itself.

Soetsu Yanagi, *The Unknown Craftsman*

… 4 …

Fibers and fiber preparation
Choose good-quality materials and prepare them well

Fiber selection and preparation are keys to good spinning. When you begin to spin, however, you need to be able to identify good fibers—not necessarily to select and prepare them yourself!

So I will limit my discussion of this subject. First among my reasons is that I think spinners new to high-whorling should concentrate on their spinning techniques, working with the high-quality prepared fibers that are available today. Whether you are working with fiber you have bought "ready to spin" or with fiber you have prepared yourself, be sure to check out the information on conditioning fibers at the end of this chapter. If you want to have the finest time spinning, you will want to condition *all* prepared fibers before you spin them.

The study of fibers is a field in and of itself. There is a lot of information in print for you to study as your skills and needs develop. Here I will cover basic information for those who are not familiar with the terms and techniques. I will also offer my approach to fiber selection and preparation, principally related to wool because that is the fiber of choice for most spinners. I will also concentrate on the use of simple hand-held tools, for these are more appropriate to high-whorling than higher-capacity studio-type equipment.

Fiber choice

All traditional fibers can be spun on a high-whorl handspindle. Because wool gives us the full range of possibilities, I will focus on its use and will add notes about some of the other fibers. Bear in mind that I am primarily a knitter and a sometime tapestry weaver, so many of my comments are directed to those uses with which I am most competent.

Long fibers

Wool and other longer fibers (flax, hemp, mohair, and so on) can be spun on a suspended spindle with ease. With these fibers, you may choose to spin with the spindle supported on your thigh either for reasons of personal comfort or because you would like to produce a softer yarn.

Short fibers

For the short, fine, and/or slick fibers (cotton, cashmere, alpaca, kid mohair, angora, and the like), use the spindle supported on your thigh. With experience, many spinners find that they can also spin these fibers using a suspended lightweight spindle, especially if the slick fiber has been blended with a small amount of wool.

Fibers and fiber preparation

Wool

Wool is the easiest fiber to spin. You can readily spin it with the spindle supported on your thigh to make a light, lofty, low-twist bulky singles for knitting sweaters or with the spindle suspended to make a high-twist, dense, sock or warp yarn—and every yarn in between.

Wools are described primarily in terms of *fiber length, fiber fineness,* and *crimp* (or the waviness of the fiber). Finely crimped fibers look like they zigzag many times between their cut end and their tip. Fibers with much less crimp may simply look slightly wavy.

Each breed of sheep grows a characteristic type of wool, and the breeds are classified into groups reflecting the similarity of the wools they produce. Wool comes in several grades, called *fine, medium, long (coarse),* and *braid.*

Fine wools are short, highly crimped fibers from sheep breeds such as Rambouillet, Merino, and Cormo. These wools are great for garments worn next to the skin. They are ideally suited for being spun into fine to medium-weight yarns, between laceweight and sportweight. Because of their crimp, which helps to absorb the twist forces, they can also be spun into knitting-worsted–weight yarns. Beginning spinners should avoid the fine wools until they are comfortable handling the spindle with medium wools. The fine wools may become your favorite fibers to spin, but there is no question that they are more difficult

Fine wools

to handle than more "average" wools, both in the fleece and as prepared fibers.

Medium wools

Medium wools are longer than the fine wools, and they have a more open crimp. Examples include Finn, Corriedale, and Columbia. These wools are easy to use and can be spun in a wide range of weights, from fine yarns to bulky singles.

Long wools

Long wools, with their very open, wavy crimp, subtle sheen, and coarser fibers, lend themselves to the making of dense, durable yarns that are suited for use in handweaving (for warp yarns and rug weft) or for knitting or crocheting garments that will experience hard wear, such as socks and outer garments.

Braid wools

Braid wools are very coarse and often hairy as well. They make great rug wools. You may find other uses for braid wools—where you want texture and durability and you don't care if the resulting fabric is scratchy.

While practicing your high-whorling skills, I suggest working with the medium wools and the finer long wools (Romney is my preference). When you are comfortable with the tools, experiment with the other wools.

Fibers in my lifestyle

I spin mostly wool. Because I live at an elevation of 6300 feet in the arid piñon-juniper landscape of the Colorado Plateau, wool is my ideal fiber. Even though we have barefoot days during the summer, the air chills rapidly as the sun sets, making a light

Fibers and fiber preparation

wool shawl and socks delightful—and my big, thick, woolly Cowichan vests and sweaters make the bright and sunny-but-cold winters a pleasure.

For fancy socks, I might choose the medium wools for soft but less sturdy socks—the kind that I use for dress wear (which to me means "good blue jeans"). Among the medium wools, I prefer Finn (caressingly soft with some sheen), Columbia (readily available in the West), and Corriedale (soft sheen and quite durable).

For everyday socks, I prefer the long wools, because they are more durable. But I usually choose individual fleeces from the finer end of the long-wool grade. My favorite long wools are a crimpy Romney or a finer Lincoln, which give me sheen, durability, and the range of natural colors that I crave.

Crossbred wools are another option. These wools come from long-term breeding programs designed to create wools with specific characteristics, not necessarily to develop a stabilized breed. I am particularly fond of Finn-Lincoln and of Karashire, a trademarked Karakul-Shropshire cross. I sometimes think of these fibers as my favorites, because they combine the best of both worlds: they have characteristics of medium and long wools, along with a good natural color range.

I also use some dual-coated wools from the primitive breeds of sheep. Dual-coated sheep grow both short, fine fibers (for warmth) and longer fibers (for protection from wild weather). Some dual-

Sock illustration by Priscilla Gibson-Roberts.

coated fleeces have a short woolly undercoat and a long silky outer coat; I like these for socks. Some dual-coated sheep grow very coarse, almost wiry, outer coats, which are great for tapestry weaving.

My natural favorite among the dual-coated breeds is the little Churro, brought into the Southwest by the early Spanish explorers—the lamb's wool is great for socks! This breed is often called Navajo-Churro; it has historically been used to weave Navajo blankets and rugs. Karakul lamb's wool can also be wonderful. The adult Karakul fleece was traditionally used by village weavers in the Middle East and Central Asia. Spelsau from Norway is also lovely. The long wool provides durability while the short woolly undercoat offers cushioning. Although people with sensitive skin might find Spelsau prickly in socks, it is unsurpassed for tapestry work.

To enhance the characteristics of a given fiber, I often blend it with other fibers. Adding a small amount of kid mohair to wool can give you socks of incredible silkiness. Blend mohair with wool to use when knitting the heels and toes of socks: they will wear unusually well and if you dye the fiber you will get a sparkle of more intense color, letting the world know that you have created something special here! For lightweight socks that are incredibly warm, blend angora and a fine wool. Yes, the angora has a tendency to felt on the inside of the sock, but this does not alter its value.

Fibers and fiber preparation

Sometimes I do not want wool socks. I want cotton socks. As a knitter, however, I am somewhat disdainful of cotton's lack of elasticity. So what can I do to have the cool comfort of cotton along with increased elasticity? I blend a small percentage of wool into the cotton. I use one of the fine wools, such as Merino, as about 20 percent of the mixture.

Fine wools are not ideal for socks because they are soft and they don't endure wear as well as the heavier wools. You can overcome this when you spin your own yarn: make the singles, two-ply the singles, then cable the two-ply—I'll tell you how to do this on page 156.

These are just a few comments about how I approach fiber choice. Experiment to find out what works for you.

Fiber preparation

Fiber preparation is the key to effortless, consistent spinning. The preparation, in combination with spinning techniques, controls many of the characteristics in the final yarn.

Even if you do not do your own preparation initially—and I suggest that you do not take on these tasks right away, because so many excellent prepared fibers are available—you will be able to select fibers more knowledgeably if you understand some of the essentials of how fibers are prepared.

There are compelling reasons why you may want to learn to prepare your own fibers: primary among them are quality and control (of source, blend, and/or color effects). But learn to spin first.

I must also emphasize that when preparing and/or conditioning fibers prior to spinning, your fiber supply must be consistent with the yarn you plan to spin. A fine yarn requires a skinny fiber supply whereas a bulky yarn requires a fat fiber supply. An overabundant or inadequately substantial fiber supply can lead to frustration and, all too often, defeat.

Woolen and worsted

In standard preparation there are two choices that apply to all fibers, not just wool: *carded* for the making of *woolen-spun yarn* and *combed* for the making of *worsted-spun yarn*. Carding and combing processes result in yarns with widely diverse characteristics, and there is a full range of gray area between pure woolen and pure worsted yarns.

In woolen yarns, the fibers are *roughly* aligned and of varying lengths. Woolen yarns tend to be fluffier, softer, and warmer than worsted yarns. In worsted yarns, the fibers are *definitely* aligned and all of about the same length. Worsted yarns tend to be sleeker, smoother, and more durable than woolen yarns.

True woolen yarns are highly regarded for their warmth and light weight. Woolen yarns are not as durable as worsted yarns. The fibers most desirable for this type of yarn are the short (4 inches

Woolen yarn

Fibers and fiber preparation

[10 cm] or less), highly crimped fibers. When spun with low twist, the fibers tend to push apart, and many of the fiber ends protrude on the yarn's surface to create a halo. This halo creates air space that enhances the air space within the core of the yarn, and all that contained air gives the yarn great insulating property. If you knit, weave, or crochet with this yarn, the halo overlaps in the spaces between the stitches or woven strands and mutes the pattern, whether you are patterning the fabric with texture or with color.

Because all the short fibers are present in the yarn and because relatively low levels of twist secure those fibers within the yarn, the shorter fibers are free to migrate to the surface to form pills. Unlike synthetic fiber pills that become shaggy and unsightly and are hard to remove, wool pills tend to form and then break off.

Carded fibers can be used to create a woolen or a worsted-type (not true worsted) yarn, depending upon the spinning technique selected.

Combed fibers are used to create worsted yarn, and with skill you can also learn to use them to make a sleek but woolen-type yarn. The combing process results in the parallel alignment of the fibers with all short fibers removed. The longer, less crimpy wools (4 inches [10 cm] or more) are considered most desirable for combing. The resulting yarn is usually spun with a relatively high level of twist, to enhance density, durability, and sheen. The fibers are twisted

Worsted yarn

Spinning in the Old Way

along their entire length (their ends don't stick out, as in woolen spinning); thus pilling is all but nonexistent. Pattern, whether produced by texture or by color, will be clear and distinct because there is no halo to obscure the edges of the yarn strands. Worsted yarns are not as warm as woolen yarns.

Because only the ends of the fibers protrude from the more highly twisted worsted yarns, people with sensitive skin may call worsted garments "prickly." In mill production, worsteds are flamed (gassed) to singe and remove the prickles. It is interesting that flaming is also possible for handcrafted yarns, although most handspinners choose softer yarns in the first place if sensitivity is a concern. In Armenia, socks knitted from yarns of coarse wools were turned inside out, wetted thoroughly, mounted on beautifully carved wooden "blockers" shaped much like the soles of the socks, then passed over a flame to remove the prickles from the portion of the sock that would touch the foot.

Woolen versus worsted—which do I prefer? Frankly, I go through spells of combing when I want only true worsted yarns. Then I will enter a hand-carding phase. At some point, I decide that no, I want drum-carded fibers (prepared on a human-powered mechanical carder).

Once you know how to do it, preparation is fast and easy. Controlling preparation allows me to shade my yarn's characteristics from soft woolen to dense worsted-type yarns.

Fibers and fiber preparation

Hand carding:
The starting point for cozy, woolen-spun yarns

Carding loosens up fibers and arranges them so that they are fluffy. If there are no clumps, then it is far easier to control the flow of the fibers while you are spinning.

Before carding, fibers are *scoured*. This term sounds more drastic than it is. Scouring involves a gentle-soak cleaning with a mild detergent and plenty of hot water. My preferred cleansing agent is an agricultural animal shampoo called Orvus, but good-quality hand dish-washing detergent will work. Then the fiber is air dried. The wool is then opened (*teased* or gently pulled apart, so the fibers are loose and not in clumps). During teasing, foreign matter drops out (seeds, straw, and other non-fiber stuff) and the wool is lofted (fluffed up).

Scouring

The final step is the actual carding. Carders work in pairs. Each carder has a face covered with carding cloth (special leather or vulcanized cloth embedded with many fine, bent steel teeth). These two faces are used in opposition to each other, and the wool is passed back and forth between the two carders in a rhythmic process that is repeated until all the fibers are in rough alignment and homogenized.

Carding

You can card with hand carders (which I use for all my fine fibers, including fine wool) or with a drum carder (good for the medium and long wools).

Hand-carded fibers

The carded fibers from the hand carders, when rolled into a tubular form called by its Scandinavian name of *rolag,* are used to spin true woolen yarns. This will produce the lightest, loftiest yarn possible. The fibers from the drum carder are usually in the form of a large batt, although some spinners have a smaller version of a drum carder that produces a roving.

Drum-carded fibers

Drum-carded fibers can be spun into a woolen yarn (somewhat more dense than the yarn spun from rolags) or as a worsted-type yarn, for greater density and durability. This won't be a true worsted yarn, but will share some of its characteristics.

Carder basics

Hand carders come with flat or curved backs. People develop different preferences. In my experience, flat-back carders with offset handles are less stressful on most people's hands.

With flat carders, use flat strokes. With curved carders, use wrist action on each stroke to follow the curved surfaces.

The key to carding is gentle movement. Your goal is to keep the fibers between the sets of teeth on the carders, not to embed the fibers into the teeth as if you were brushing hair.

Fibers and fiber preparation

Basics of hand carding

Loading the carder

1. Hold one carder with the cloth side facing up. Lightly load the carder with fiber by stroking teased fibers gently across the surface so their ends catch lightly on the metal teeth. This is the bottom carder. It stays relatively still while you work.

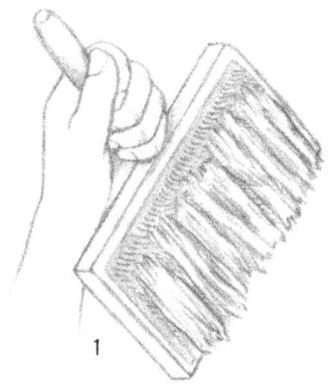

Stroking

2. Stroke the top carder over the bottom carder in progressive passes, beginning with a movement that delicately engages only the fibers on the lower third of the bottom carder (measuring from the side without the handle). On each subsequent stroke, add one-third of the bottom carder.

The fiber will gradually transfer from the bottom carder to the top carder. Three passes are usually sufficient, although one or two extras are okay.

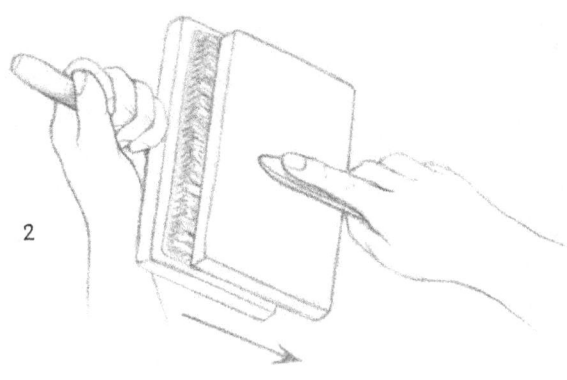

Disengaging the fiber from the carders

3. With the carding cloth facing up on both carders, transfer the fibers from the top carder to the bottom carder.

Do this by placing the top carder one-third of the way down the bottom carder (measuring from the handle). Lightly press the teeth of the two carders together to catch the fringe of the

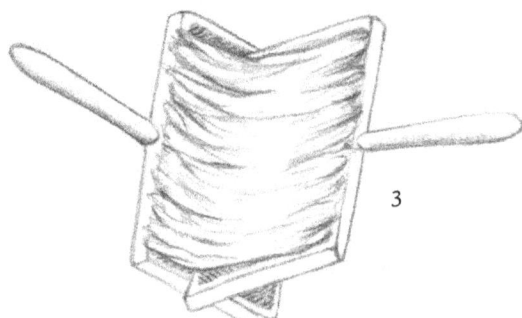

fiber on the top carder in the teeth of the bottom carder.

LIFT UP with the bottom carder and the fibers will lift off the top carder and rest across the bottom carder.

4. Again with the carding cloth facing up on both carders, transfer the fiber from the bottom carder to the top carder.

Do this by placing the bottom carder one-third of the way down on the top carder (the bottom carder is now on top, and you are measuring one-third from the handle end). Lightly press the two carders together so the fringe of fiber catches on the teeth of the now-bottom carder. LIFT UP again

Fibers and fiber preparation

> **Batt**
> The fibers remain in a flat mass, as you lift them from the carders.
>
> **Roving**
> Using the carder as a platform, fold the batt in half, fold it in half again, and then gently elongate the mass.
>
> **Rolag**
> Roll the fibers gently into a cylinder that parallels the long edge of the carder.

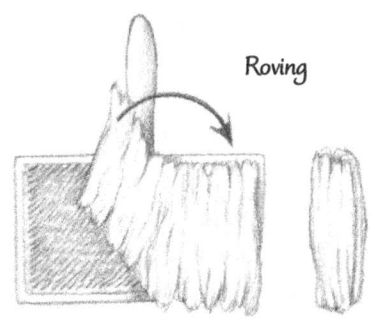

with the bottom carder to transfer the fiber to the top.

If necessary, continue carding from top to bottom, then bottom to top. I frequently make three passes in each direction.

You are done when the fibers have all been separated from each other and the mass of fibers has an even density.

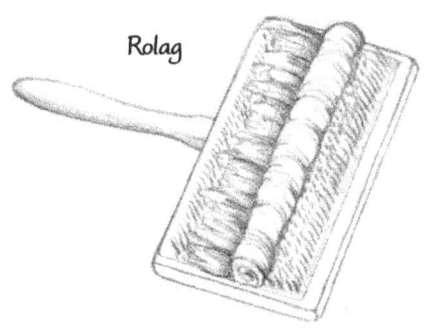

To completely remove fibers from carders, lift from the top and then from the bottom, as in steps 3 and 4 on the previous page.

Then choose whether you would like your fibers in a *batt*, a *roving*, or a *rolag*.

Spinning in the Old Way

Peasant combing: Straight and sleek

Combing is a more precise fiber preparation technique than carding. In addition to loosening the fibers, it leaves them arranged so they lie parallel to each other and it removes the shortest fibers. Combed fibers are therefore not only aligned but are all of approximately the same length.

There are many types of combs, and like carders they are used in pairs. I like what are called peasant combs, because they are lightweight and easy to store and use. They have one row of teeth or tines on each comb.

For combing, the wool is cleansed in a way that maintains the lock structure of the wool. Some spinners scour lock by lock, one at a time. Others carefully layer the fleece in the scouring bath, keeping the locks precisely oriented while they wash batches of wool.

Washing wool for combing

After the wool locks are clean, they are lightly opened and then mounted on hand-held combs. During combing, the locks are passed from the stationary comb to the moving comb, then the process is reversed and repeated as many times as necessary until the fibers are all open and of the same length. All short fibers and foreign matter will be retained on the comb and will be discarded. The wool is then drawn off the comb into a long strand called a *top*.

Open, comb, and draw off top

Fibers and fiber preparation

Basics of peasant combing

1. Loading

Load one comb with clean, open locks until one-third to one-half of the length of the tines are filled. Load the locks by catching just a bit of one end of each lock in the tines.

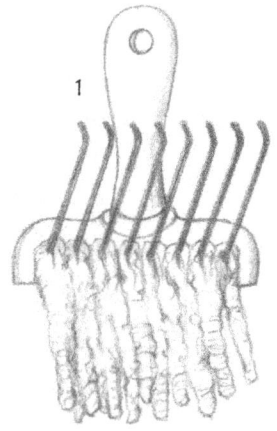

I like to lay down a thin layer of locks mounted by their cut ends, followed by a thin layer mounted by their tip ends. Loading in this manner lets me forget about spinning a "directional" yarn (all tip ends running in the same direction throughout processing and spinning).

Be sure to catch only the ends of the locks, so most of the length of each fiber hangs free.

One comb will be the moving comb and one will be the stationary comb in the steps that follow. The fibers will pass back and forth between them. This loaded comb will start as the stationary comb.

2 & 3. Combing

Imagine you are looking DOWN on the combs in drawings 2 and 3. The stationary comb (shown in profile on the left) should face away from you as you work. The moving comb (shown on the right in each drawing) will face down.

2. Take the moving comb down through the fringe of fibers, beginning with the loose ends and working progressively upward into the fiber with each pass.

As you do this, fibers will transfer to the moving comb. Short fibers and debris will remain on the stationary comb. When you have combed as much as you can onto the moving comb, clean the short leftovers from the stationary comb.

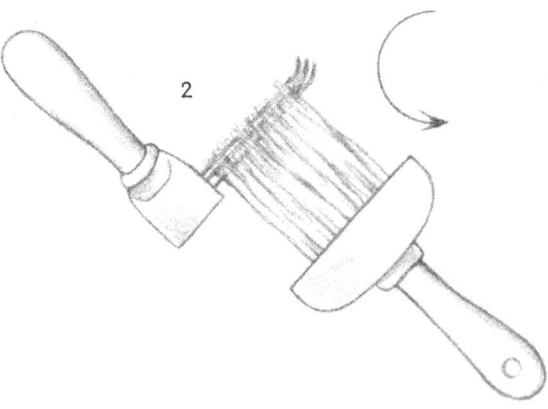

Fibers and fiber preparation

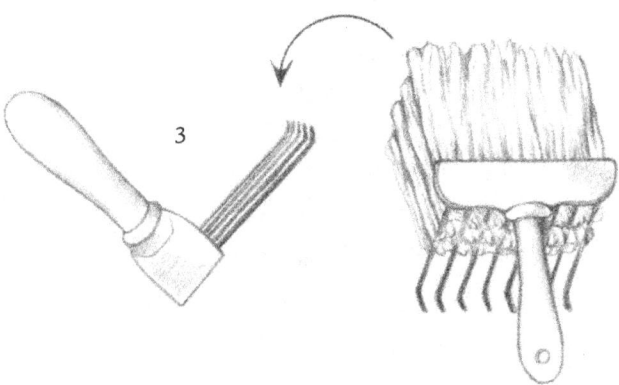

3. Now pass fibers from the moving comb back onto the stationary comb. To do this, you change your hand movements, not the positions of the combs.

Again begin at the fringe and work more deeply into the mass of fiber with each pass. The fibers will transfer back to the stationary comb. Clean the debris and short fibers off of the moviug comb.

Repeat steps 2 and 3 until the fibers are smooth, fully aligned, and free of debris and short bits.

4. Drawing the fiber off the comb

To form the combed fiber into top for spinning worsted yarn, stabilize the comb that holds the fiber when you are finished. Here the comb has been placed on a wooden pad with a post.

With your hand, stroke the fibers toward their free ends to form a point.

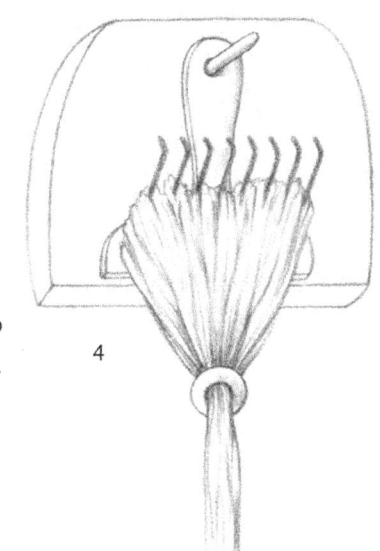

Spinning in the Old Way

Thread this point through a volume gauge; the traditional gauge is called a *diz*. You can use any object that you can hold easily that has a smooth hole in it. The size of the hole will relate directly to the size of yarn you intend to spin.

Draw the fiber through the volume gauge, working hand over hand in small increments so the strand of fiber remains continuous and is consistent in density.

Form a bird's nest, as described on the next page, to keep the top in order until you are ready to spin.

Storing prepared fibers

Batt
Roving
Rolag
Top
Bird's nest

When the fibers have been prepared, you will need to store them until you want to spin them. There are several "packages" in which you can safely store prepared fibers. (Batts, rovings, and rolags are illustrated on page 77.)

1. *Batts:* flat sheets of carded fibers prepared on hand carders or a drum carder.

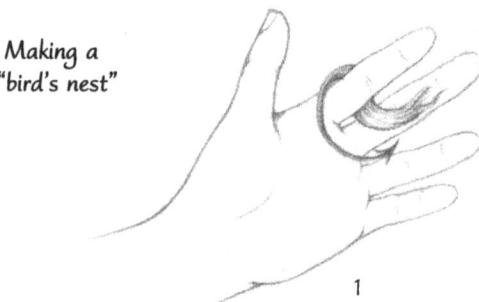

Making a "bird's nest"

1

Fibers and fiber preparation

2. *Roving:* batts condensed to form a long, fairly dense strip with just a hint of twist added to maintain integrity; the strips are rolled into loose balls for storage.

3. *Rolags:* carded fibers rolled into a tubular form.

4. *Top:* combed fibers drawn out in a long strip that is rolled and stored like a roving.

5. *Bird's nest:* hand-combed top, wrapped around your hand with a circular motion; then the end is tucked in to secure it.

Making a "bird's nest" from top or roving

1. Tuck one end between your first two fingers. Wrap the strand of fiber around the first two fingers two or three times.

2. Add your third finger to the group and continue to wrap; go around two or three times.

3. Add your fourth finger and finish the wrapping, going around as many times as you need to. Tuck in the loose end to secure it. Slip the bundle of fiber off your hand and store it.

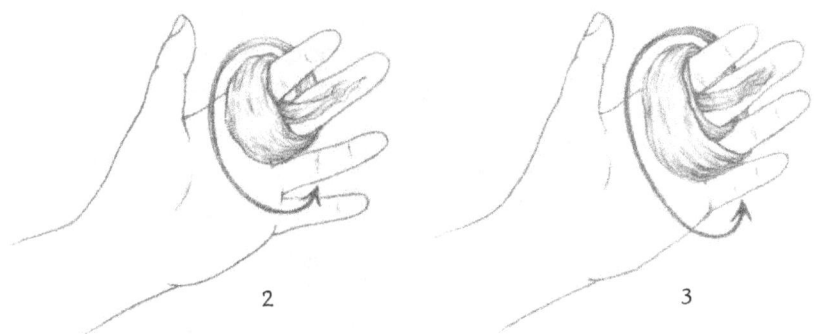

When you are ready to spin, pull the fiber from the center of the bird's nest—begin with the end that you started with in step 1.

Conditioning fibers

After storage, the fibers must be conditioned before you spin them. The rolag and the bird's nest need the least attention—at most a little shake to increase their loft.

Even when I have hand carded the fiber, I like a roving more than rolags for my spindle work. To make a roving from a hand-carded batt, I fold the fibers in half across the face of the batt, then repeat the folding once more (see illustration on page 77). I elongate this folded bundle just like the larger drum-carded batts described below.

Converting a drum-carder batt to rovings

The thick batts off large drum carders need a good shake or two to loft them. Next, you'll divide each batt into strips that can be elongated.

Divide the batt

1. Divide the batt into two halves. Begin at the center and move gently to each end in turn. Repeat with each half, so you end up with four sections of about the same size.

To divide a batt, encircle each side with a hand, meeting in the middle to pinch and draw apart.

Fibers and fiber preparation

Move gently to each end in turn, making two sections from the original one.

Repeat this process on each half so that you end up with four sections of about the same size.

Elongate each section

2. Then elongate each quarter. With hands slightly apart (just a bit more than the distance of the length of one of the fibers in the batt), grasp the strip in both hands and gently tug, using a gentle tug-and-release motion to keep from pulling the fibers completely apart. Start at one end and move slowly toward the other end, working to keep the amount of fiber evenly distributed. Grasp one hand at the end of the area just elongated while the other moves up.

Continue in this manner until the whole strip has been elongated. Sometimes a batt requires more than one pass at elongating.

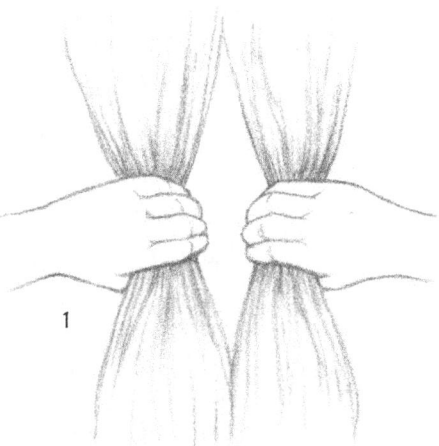

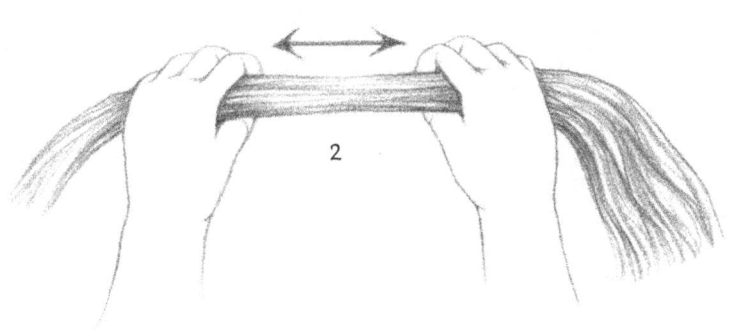

Spinning in the Old Way

Conditioning roving—
especially good for commercially prepared fiber

Commercial roving, whether carded or combed, needs special attention because the fibers end up quite densely packed together, when compared to hand prepared fibers.

Divide a section of roving lengthwise

1. Pull off a length of roving that measures about 36 to 45 inches (91 to 114 cm). (Longer sections are unwieldy to control when spinning.) First grasp one end and shake it vigorously; then repeat the shaking from the other end. This loosens the fibers.

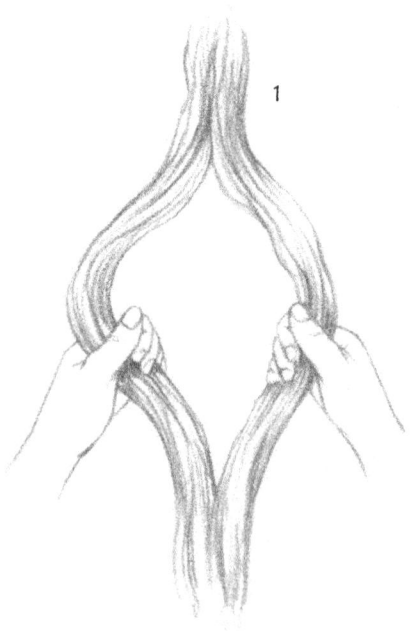

Beginning at its middle and working toward each end in turn, gently separate this section into two even parts. Re-divide the parts if you would like thinner sections; you will want thin sections if you plan to spin thin yarn, and thick sections if you plan to spin thick yarn.

Fibers and fiber preparation

Elongate each strip
2. Starting at one end, elongate the fibers between your hands. The process is similar to the way you would elongate a batt (page 85, step 2), but you will have some snap in your tug-and-release movements, in order to fluff and open the compressed fibers.

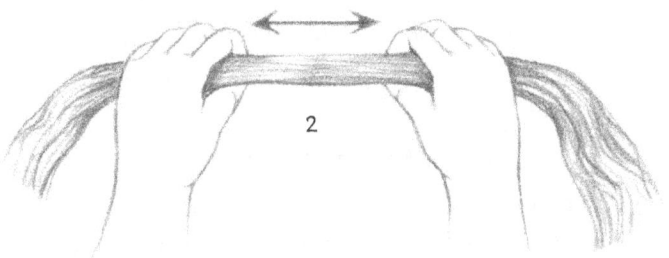

Where to put the fiber when you are ready to spin it

Once they have been conditioned, the fibers are ready to spin. Rolags need only be readily accessible to the spinner, because they are small packages. But the other forms are now long strips that will interfere with your spinning unless they are somehow contained.

In many parts of the world, the fibers are put onto a long-handled holder (called a *distaff*) that is held under the arm or secured in a waistband or belt.

Distaff

I much prefer the Eastern nomadic tradition of coiling roving on the arm. During spinning, one hand controls the spindle, inserting the twist, while

Coiling fiber on the arm

the other hand controls the fiber supply. I use my right hand for the spindle, my left for the fibers.

Coiling roving or top on your arm, for ease in spinning

Start by tucking one end of the fiber strand under anything near your wrist—a bracelet, watchband, shirtsleeve, rubber band, or sweater cuff will do. This will prevent the dangling end of the strip from catching in the yarn as you spin. I use my Navajo storyteller bracelet.

Then wrap the fiber loosely around your arm.

I coil the strip around my arm counterclockwise, with the end coming out at my thumb. I prefer counterclockwise winding because I am most comfortable flicking my wrist clockwise to release a new section of fiber.

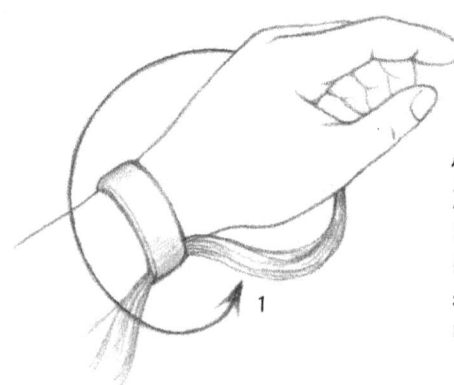

Alternative 1, fiber wrapped counterclockwise

I prefer to wrap counterclockwise, because I can quickly release a new section of fiber with an easy flick of my wrist.

Fibers and fiber preparation

Other spinners prefer to wrap the length of fiber around the arm clockwise, with the strip coming off the little-finger side of the hand. This keeps the bulk of the fiber strip farther from the twisting spindle, so the unspun fiber is less likely to get accidentally caught in the developing yarn.

Others randomly wrap, clockwise or counterclockwise, because it matters little to them.

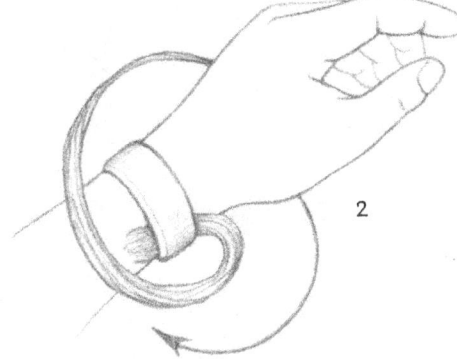

Alternative 2, fiber wrapped clockwise
If you wrap clockwise, the fiber will be kept farther from the spinning zone and will be less likely to catch in the developing yarn.

THE PRINCIPLE OF BEAUTY OF CRAFT IS NO DIFFERENT FROM THE LAW THAT RULES THE SPIRIT UNDERLYING ALL THINGS.

Soetsu Yanagi, *The Unknown Craftsman*

5

Spinning technique
Discover methods that will work for you

A high-whorl spindle is incredibly versatile. You can spin with it either suspended or supported, to produce a full range of woolen and worsted yarns.

By *suspended*, I mean that the handspindle hangs from the newly created yarn while you continue to extend its length. Many refer to a spindle used in this manner as a *drop spindle*. I prefer the more descriptive term *suspended spindle* because of the unfortunate connotation that "drop" carries. You can either stand or sit when using the handspindle in this manner.

Suspended

Supported means that the shaft rests on something, in this case on your thigh. This way the yarn does not have to support the weight of the handspindle. Spinning is done while seated. In some parts of the world a supported high-whorl spindle is referred to as a *lap spindle*.

Supported

A supported spindle is ideal for making soft woolen yarns and the big, bulky singles that are so hard to spin on a wheel, while a suspended spindle lends itself to spinning denser woolen and high-twist worsted yarns.

For both techniques, I personally prefer to spin while seated on my slanted-seat weaver's bench or a stool.

Direction of rotation

Z twist and S twist

A handspindle can rotate in either of two possible directions. The resulting strand is known as either Z-twist or S-twist yarn, depending on the direction in which the spindle rotates.

Rolling the shaft of the handspindle clockwise results in a Z-twisted yarn. The angle of twist on the yarn will match the center portion of the letter Z.

Conversely, rolling the shaft counterclockwise results in an S-twisted yarn. The angle of twist will match the center portion of the letter S.

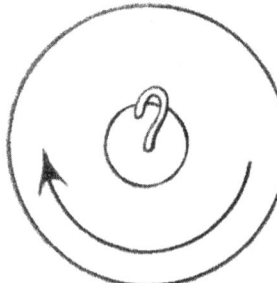

Clockwise rotation

Clockwise rotation, as viewed from the top of the handspindle, results in a Z twist.

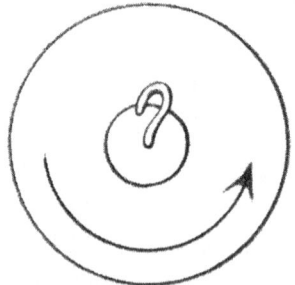

Counterclockwise rotation

Counterclockwise rotation, as viewed from the top of the handspindle, results in an S twist.

Spinning technique

And how do I determine what is clockwise and what is counter-clockwise? By looking down onto the top of the whorl. If the top of the whorl is turning clockwise, you will make a Z yarn. If the top of the whorl is turning counter-clockwise, you will make an S yarn.

As a general rule, singles are spun Z and then plied yarns are spun S. This is true for knitting yarns, whereas yarns spun for crochet are best constructed with S singles, Z plied. In crochet, the wrapping action of yarn around the hook removes the S twist. After crocheting with S-plied yarn for a while, you might find yourself with the separate strands instead of an integrated yarn.

There are many ways to use S- and Z-twist strands for design effects, in both the finished yarn and in a fabric. Some weavers like to spin both S and Z singles, then play them against each other on the loom to produce textural effects.

Z-spun yarn

A Z twist in the yarn results when the spindle is turned clockwise. Most singles are spun in this manner.

S-spun yarn

An S twist in the yarn results when the spindle is turned counter-clockwise. Most yarns are plied in this manner.

Here's an extra tip: If you are spinning a balanced-ply yarn, when the yarn is balanced the fibers in the Z-twisted singles will end up parallel to the center of the yarn (as shown in the lower drawing).

Spinning in the Old Way

Positions for rolling the spindle on your leg

Spinning comfortably

As we explored in chapter 2, you can spin with the spindle either hanging free (suspended) or with its weight resting on the thigh (supported). There are several options for how you roll the spindle, and my preferences are based on good body mechanics: so it is possible to spin comfortably for as long as you want to.

Rolling the spindle on the OUTSIDE of your leg and the resulting twist directions

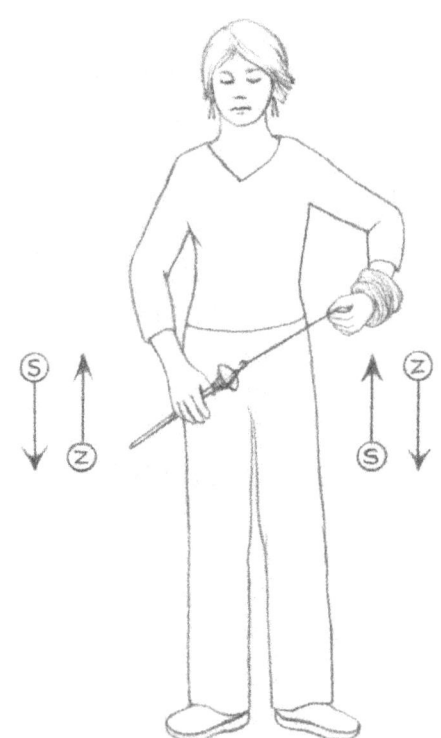

Standing position:
spindle hangs free
(suspended spinning method)

Sitting position:
spindle rests on thigh
(supported spinning method)

For Z twist, roll UP on the outside of your right thigh or DOWN on the outside of your left thigh.

For S twist, roll DOWN on the outside of your right thigh or UP on the outside of your left thigh.

Spinning technique

Spinning while standing

When standing, you'll be spinning with the spindle suspended and you'll roll the shaft on the outside of your leg. You can roll it on either the right side or on the left side, for either S or Z twist.

On the right side, roll the shaft up your thigh for Z and down your leg for S. On the left side, roll the shaft down your thigh for Z and up your thigh for S.

Spinning while sitting down

When seated, you can work with the spindle either supported or suspended.

Spindle in supported position

When I am spinning with the spindle in a supported position, the rotational directions for the spindle are the same as when I spin in a standing position. I roll the spindle along the outside of my right thigh, drawing the fibers to the left across my lap, in order to maintain spinal alignment.

Spindle suspended

When spinning by the suspended method while seated, I spread my legs and roll the spindle along the inside of my left thigh because this allows me to maintain good spinal alignment. If I were to work on the outside of my thigh, I would need to twist my spine to get my arms into position. See the next page for an illustration of this alternative.

You'll recall that my dress-up clothing consists of my "good" blue jeans! I'm always ready to spin.

Spinning in the Old Way

Tips for smooth, fast rolling

When you are rolling the spindle up your leg, begin the roll with the heel of your hand and when you reach your fingertips, give the spindle a flip with your fingers to maximize its rotational speed. When you are rolling the spindle down your leg, begin the rotation with the tips of your fingers, pushing off at the end with the heel of your hand to give the spindle a boost of speed.

You can use any combination of the up- and down-rolling positions that is comfortable. This

Rolling the spindle on the INSIDE of your leg and the resulting twist directions

Sitting position:
spindle rolls on inside of thigh and then hangs directly in front of the body for drafting
(suspended spinning method)

For Z twist, roll DOWN on the inside of your right thigh or UP on the inside of your left thigh.

For S twist, roll UP on the inside of your right thigh or DOWN on the inside of your left thigh.

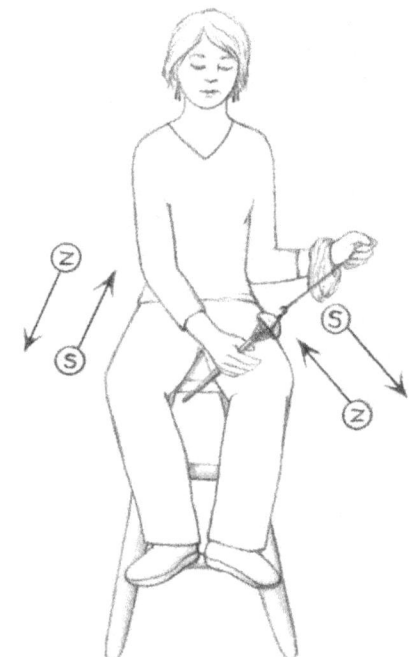

Spinning technique

means that you can do all the rolling on your right side, by coming up for Z and going down for S. Or you can do all the rolling on your left side, down for Z and up for S. You can also roll up on the right side for Z and up on the left side for S, or, alternatively, down on the left for Z and on the right for S.

I have tried the various combinations. I prefer the upward roll on either right or left. This means that the hand that controls the spindle shifts from right to left. In other words, when I am spinning Z-twist singles, I hold and control the handspindle with my right hand and the fibers with my left hand. When plying in S-twist direction, I control the spindle with my left hand and the fiber (in this case, singles yarns) in my right hand. I have found this to be most comfortable because each arm performs similar activities.

My preferences: a mixture

Working this way has another advantage. Most of the spinning is Z singles, so during most of my spinning time I can free my right hand in a split second by releasing the handspindle. This means that I can drop the spindle quickly to stir the boiling pot, grab the wayward child, answer the telephone, or attend to any other need that comes up. When the fibers are wrapped around my hand, freeing that hand is more complicated. When I ply off the nostepinne, as I usually do and as I will teach you to do (pages 151 to 153), I have no problem freeing either hand when necessary.

Spinning in the Old Way

Beginning the yarn

There are two ways to begin your yarn, that is, to attach those first fibers to the handspindle. One requires the use of a leader, which is similar to the method described in chapter 2 (pages 32–33), and the other lets you begin directly with the fiber itself.

Using a leader

I use this technique when I plan to pull the yarn from the center of the cop. The brightly colored leader eliminates any confusion about what to pull out.

Attach leader

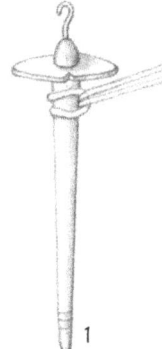

1. Break off about a 36-inch (91-cm) length of brightly colored, fairly fine, plied yarn.

The technique that I use to attach the leader when beginning to actually spin differs slightly from the technique that I use for practice "spinning." It leaves an open loop to which I attach the fibers.

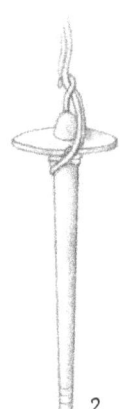

Fold the yarn over at its middle and tie the ends together with an overhand knot. Lay this knot against the shaft of the spindle and draw the free end of the loop through the knotted end. This free end will be available as the place from which to start spinning. I also add a half-hitch just under the spindle whorl to ensure that the leader will not slip.

2. Take the leader through the notch on the whorl and then up through the hook.

You're ready to spin.

Spinning technique

Join fiber

3. Draw out the fibers at the end of the fiber supply, tuck a few through the loop, then turn the spindle's shaft to insert twist. When the fibers are securely joined to the leader with a short section of newly spun yarn, wind the leader (and the new yarn, if it's long enough) onto the shaft. Wind on in the same direction as you are turning the spindle when you spin.

Beginning without a leader

The second way to start begins with the fibers themselves, and no leader.

Fan out the fibers and catch a few with the spindle hook

1. Fan out the fibers with the hand that you will use to control them (I use my left hand). Do this while holding the tip of the supply between your first and second fingers and holding the roving end between the thumb and the remaining two fingers of that hand.

With the handspindle in your other hand (I use my right), catch some of the fibers from the fanned-out section onto the hook. At this point, the hook is at a 90-degree angle to the fibers.

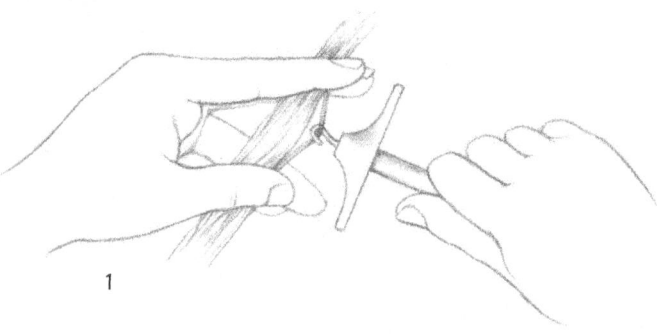

1

Rotate the spindle with your fingers and begin to spin
2. Turn the shaft between your fingers in the proper direction—in most cases, this will be clockwise—and develop a short length of yarn by rotating the spindle with your hand. Continue to rotate until you have an inch or two (2.5 to 5 cm) of yarn.

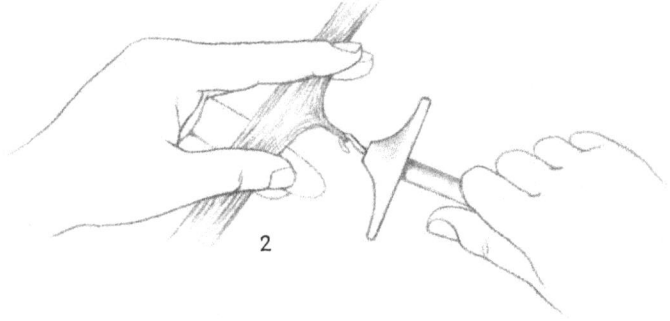

Swing the spindle so it's in a straight line with the fiber
3. As the twist begins to form the yarn, slowly shift the handspindle upward, toward the tip of the fiber supply, until the shaft is in a straight line with, and off the end of, the fiber supply.

Spinning technique

Rotate the spindle on your leg and draft a length
4. When the yarn is a foot or so long, begin to rotate the shaft on your leg while you draft out a full length of yarn.

Wind on
5. When you have spun a strand about a yard (a meter) long, pinch the end of the new yarn that's on the hook and slip the strand off the hook's tip.

Wind the yarn around the shaft of the spindle under the whorl, turning the spindle in the same direction that you have been rotating it while you have been spinning.

Continue spinning
6. Take the newly spun yarn up through the hook in the same way that you would use a leader yarn (page 98). Continue spinning.

Fine points of winding and securing the yarn

After the yarn is attached to the shaft, it passes through a notch to the hook. To maintain proper tension during spinning, you will need to keep the spindle turning in the same direction (1) when you insert twist, (2) when you wind yarn onto the shaft, and (3) when you secure the yarn onto the hook.

Keep spinning in the same direction

Winding the yarn onto the shaft

To wind the yarn onto the shaft after you have spun a comfortable length, grasp the base of the shaft and turn the whorl away from your body. This quick

Spinning in the Old Way

reverse turn (counterclockwise if you are spinning clockwise, and vice versa) will release the yarn from the hook.

With your hand still at the base of the shaft and the whorl away from your body, wind the yarn onto the shaft by rotating the spindle. Be sure to wind on in the same direction that you have been spinning (clockwise in this case). If you wind on in the opposite direction, the cop will become sloppy as the shaft fills with yarn.

Wind in the same direction

If you *wind the yarn around* the shaft, instead of *turning the shaft,* the yarn will be more securely held in place.

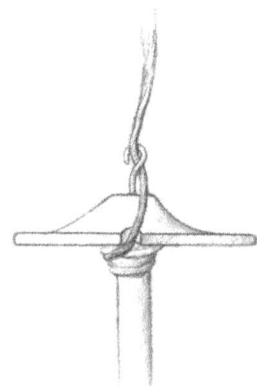

Securing yarn to hook

Depending on the location of the notches, the yarn will wrap between one-half and one full turn around the hook—a secure, yet quick-release, method of preparing to spin.

Catching yarn under hook

This works when there are notches on each side of the hook. I prefer the wrap on the hook (left), because the yarn is less likely to come off the hook accidentally.

Through the notch and onto the hook

Now you are ready with one turn of the shaft to take the yarn through the notch and onto the hook again. I leave 2 to 3 inches (5 to 7.5 cm) of spun yarn above the hook and I start drafting before I rotate the shaft. This gives me time to get my hands in position for drafting before the new twist builds up in the already-spun yarn above the hook.

Securing the yarn or catching the yarn

You can choose to secure the yarn to the hook or to catch the yarn under the hook. In the "secure" method the yarn is caught in a notch and then goes around the base of the hook before it exits upward through

---

A full turn or a partial turn?

I said that you will rotate the spindle "one turn" in order to secure the yarn to the hook. Exactly how far you turn your spindle will depend on where its notches are located and how much security you like.

You'll take the yarn one complete turn to secure it on the hook only when the notch is directly in front of the hook. This is true regardless of the direction you are spinning, either Z or S.

If the notch is directly behind the hook opening, you will only need to take one-half turn, again for both Z and S.

If the notch is to the right of the hook opening, you will take three-quarters of a turn when you are spinning Z and one and one-quarter turns when you are spinning S. The opposite is true if the notch is to the left of the hook opening: three-quarters of a turn for S and one and one-quarter turns for Z.

When the spindle has a notch on each side of the hook, some spinners simply catch the yarn under the hook (opposite page, bottom right). This brings us back to the matter of how secure you want to feel.

the eye of the hook. In the "catch" method, the yarn goes straight from the notch to the eye of the hook.

I prefer the "secure" method, with its older, traditional half-wrap of the yarn around the hook. The yarn is far less likely to come off the hook when the spindle is bumped or tension on the yarn is released.

Moving right along:
The whole spinning process at once

Here is the entire spinning process, step by step, for a Z-spun yarn.

1. Begin by spinning the first section of yarn, either with or without a leader, rotating the shaft clockwise by hand.

2. Wind onto the shaft clockwise.

3. Take the yarn through the notch, then onto the hook with a clockwise turn, leaving 2 to 3 inches (5 to 7.5 cm) of spun yarn above the hook.

4. Pre-draft a small section of fiber, allowing the twist to travel into the fibers you have drafted.

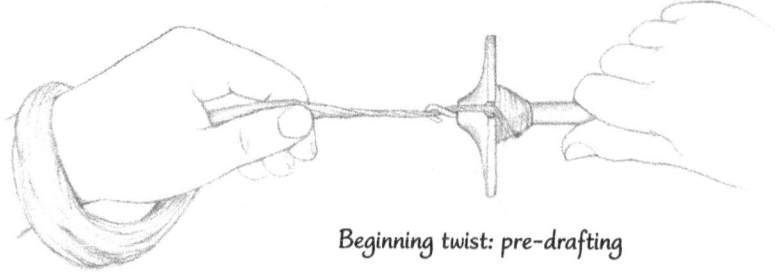

Beginning twist: pre-drafting

Spinning technique

5. Roll the shaft on your thigh. When you release the shaft and let the spindle rotate while it is suspended from the new yarn, quickly move your first (often right) hand into position to control the advancing twist. This will release your second (often left) hand to draft more fiber.

6. Draft yarn. One hand controls the flow of the twist as the other controls the flow of the fibers. Spun yarn passes over your cupped fingers down to the suspended spindle.

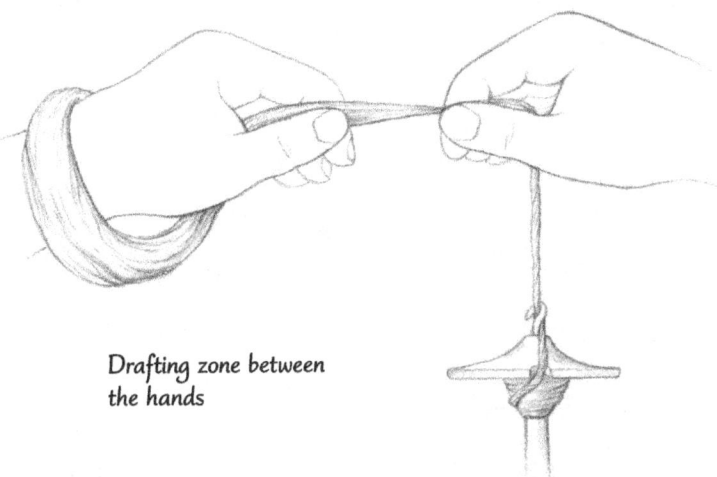

Drafting zone between the hands

7. Turning the whorl away from your body, remove the yarn from the hook with a counterclockwise turn.

8. Wind the yarn onto the shaft clockwise. Repeat steps 3 through 8 to produce a full cop of yarn.

Spinning in the Old Way

Fine points of aligning your hands

One additional concern for all spinners is proper alignment of the hands. Avoid working with your wrists bent. Even slightly bending your wrists can lead to trouble in time. You can reduce fatigue and prevent damage from repetitive motion by maintaining careful alignment.

When you spin, both your drafting hand and the hand controlling the flow of twist should be in neutral positions. "Neutral position" means that the hand is at rest, with a straight line from mid-arm to the V of the thumb and forefinger, with the fingers slightly crooked.

Keep both hands in neutral position

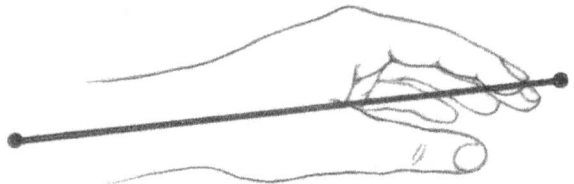

The alignment of the hands

Building the cop

Generally speaking, there are two ways to build a cop: (1) in a beehive shape, typical of Eastern spinning, or (2) in a spiraling cone, typical of Western spinning. If it suits your working style, you can build the cop through a hybrid shape that combines the beehive and the cone.

I prefer the beehive method, because I find I can wind more yarn onto the handspindle without

Spinning technique

affecting its balance. The beehive shape also allows me to ply from the center of the cop.

Basic beehive-style cop

The beehive cop is shaped like an inverted beehive. The basic shape is built from the top down.

To form it, first wind the yarn at the base of the whorl and then down the shaft, laying each strand next to the one before it, until the previously spun yarn has been covered. Make a couple of extra turns to wind the yarn onto the exposed shaft before you reverse and wind upward to the whorl.

Sometimes the yarn at the bottom of the beehive shape becomes loose. With practice, this softening of the lower portion of the cop is seldom a problem, but you can do several things to either prevent or control any looseness that does develop.

In the interest of prevention, from time to time I will spiral the yarn upward (or down, if you prefer) along the mass of yarn, instead of winding the strands side by side.

If you discover that the bottom of your beehive is becoming loose, the next time you reach the base of the cop you can wind the yarn around the shaft instead of turning the shaft to wind the yarn on, and then spiral upward. Winding around the shaft always makes a tighter wrap than turning the shaft to wind on.

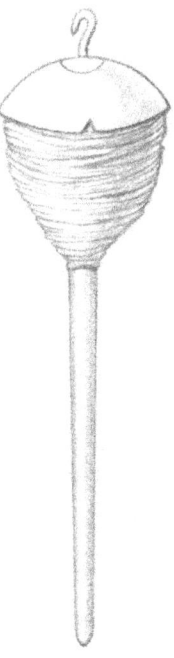

Beehive
This is typical of Eastern spinners' yarn-winding technique.

Another technique that works to tighten the lower portion involves crisscrossing the soft area, spiraling up and then down several times.

High-capacity beehive

An interesting variation of the beehive, for those who like to pack a lot of yarn onto a spindle, requires building an oval shape slightly below the whorl (rather than directly at the base of the whorl). This shape can accommodate a very heavy load of yarn. You wind the yarn up and down the shaft, until you reach the base of the whorl. Then you continue winding, extending the point of the cop at the same time that you fill in at the base of the whorl.

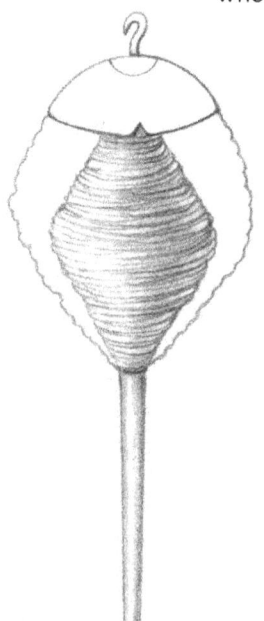

High-capacity beehive
←«

The initial buildup (dark) and the final shape (light outline) of a winding method for spinners who want the longest possible continuous strand.

Cone
»→

This is the way many Western spinners wind their yarn onto the spindle shaft.

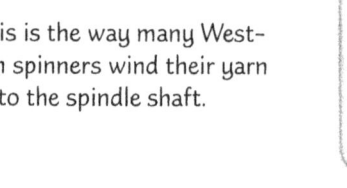

Spinning technique

Cone-shaped cop

You can make a more elongated, cone-shaped cop. Proponents of this method say there is less danger of tangles, especially when removing the yarn from the shaft. Spiral the yarn down around the shaft to the anticipated length of the cone, then spiral back up. On your next pass, spiral down again but stop one yarn wrap sooner, then turn to spiral upward. The cone builds from the bottom up—just the opposite of the beehive.

Drawing: How you use your arms

Although spinners often use the terms *draw* and *draft* interchangeably, for clarity I will use *draw* to describe the manner in which you use your arms. *Drafting* will refer to the way you elongate the fibers between your hands.

Vertical draw

When spinning with the handspindle suspended, most people advocate a vertical draw, the Western method. The fiber-supply hand is above the spindle hand, and once the hand that rotates the spindle is free it controls the flow of twist from the spindle up toward the fibers.

Vertical draw

Spinning in the Old Way

I find this method physically tiring to my arms and neck. My arms are continually extended higher and higher above my head, so I cock my head farther and farther back to see the yarn. This is especially a problem for those who have reached the age of eyeglasses with multi-focal lenses.

Horizontal draw

I much prefer the horizontal draw, which I discovered while studying photographs of Eastern spinners. My arms remain in a relaxed position, with the lower arm halfway between elbow and shoulder, which reduces the physical stress on both arms and back. The drawing remains at one comfortable focal level, eliminating the chin-up position of the vertical draw.

The spindle is suspended from the hand that controls the flow of twist. The newly spun yarn passes across the crook of the fingers, hanging off the little finger in my case. Working in this manner provides extra insurance against breaking off the yarn and dropping the spindle.

Horizontal draw

Spinning technique

When the spindle is in a supported position, my draw is at a slight angle above the horizontal, so the hand that controls the fiber supply is in about the same position as it is when the spindle is in a suspended position.

Angular draw

Between these extremes is the angular draw, a blending of the horizontal and vertical methods. Some prefer to work at an angle when they want to spin a long strand before winding on, because this position lets you comfortably extend the span between your hands.

Angular draw

Drafting:
How you elongate the fiber between your hands

The manner in which you draft the fiber, or elongate it between your hands, determines whether you are spinning *woolen* or *worsted*. Woolen yarns tend to be fluffy and soft-surfaced, and worsted yarns tend to be sleek and smooth-surfaced. Pure woolen yarns are spun from carded fibers using a woolen drafting technique. Pure worsted yarns are spun from combed fibers using a worsted drafting technique. Many yarns fall somewhere in between these pure types.

Woolen and worsted

The main difference between woolen and worsted drafting techniques involves the control of twist. Neither woolen nor worsted is superior—they are just different.

When you spin woolen (called the *long draw*), drafting the fibers and advancing the twist are simultaneous actions. When you spin worsted (called a *short draw*), drafting and twisting are separate actions, with all the drafting completed before the twist advances.

Long draw and short draw

A supported handspindle is suited to making woolen-style yarns, especially those with low twist destined to be knitted as singles. Suspended spinning is good for making worsted yarns or somewhat denser woolen yarns.

Supported and suspended

Although, as I mentioned above, carded fibers are usually spun woolen and combed fibers are usually

Spinning technique

spun worsted, your decision on the drafting technique to use should be based on what fibers you are spinning, how those fibers have been prepared, and the characteristics that you want your final yarn to have. You can spin carded fibers worsted if you would like to produce a more dense and durable yarn. Conversely, you can spin combed fibers woolen if you would like a softer, more lofty yarn.

Spin for the yarn YOU want

Woolen drafting, or long draw

There are two ways to spin woolen, both classified as the woolen or long draw: (1) spin a yarn of the desired diameter while drafting against the advancing twist, or (2) quickly elongate a loosely twisted roving and then attenuate it to the desired diameter while the twist is allowed to advance. When you work with a suspended spindle, the practical technique is the first, staying ahead of the twist. When you work with a supported spindle, you can use either method.

Two types of woolen draw

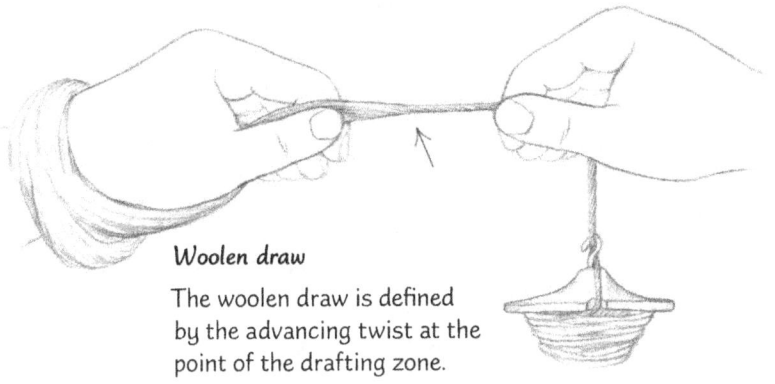

Woolen draw

The woolen draw is defined by the advancing twist at the point of the drafting zone.

In both methods, the fibers are drawn away from the handspindle. The newly spun yarn passes through the stationary hand, which controls the twist, and the yarn rests on the fingers to support the weight of the spindle. This auxiliary support, possible in horizontal drafting, allows the spinner to use woolen drafting with a suspended spindle.

The loftiest woolen yarns are spun from rolags (this is often referred to as true woolen spinning), but I prefer to spin the longer spans possible with a carded roving.

Worsted drafting, or short draw

Short draw: many opinions

There is considerable argument about what exactly is a worsted draw. And there is no definitive answer, since the reply depends upon which "expert" you are emulating, whether contemporary or historical.

All agree that worsted drafting is a short-draw technique in which the twist is held back and is not allowed to enter the drafting zone until all drafting is complete. To ensure that the yarn develops with a smooth surface, the fingers controlling the flow of twist slide along the newly spun yarn as the twist enters it. Beyond that, the picture gets cloudy.

First worsted-method opinion

One school of thought insists that you must draw the fibers out of the fiber supply with the first hand (toward the spindle), then slide the fingers back (toward the fiber supply) to slick down the fiber ends while the twist enters the yarn behind the

Spinning technique

fingers. In this case, the stationary second hand holds the fiber supply while the first hand moves to and fro.

If you let any twist enter the drafting zone, you may develop a slub, or unintentional bump, at the point where the finished yarn meets the drafting zone. If this happens, remember that you can release enough twist to eliminate the problem by applying a quick backward roll to the yarn between your thumb and finger and swiftly drafting out the lump.

When you work with a suspended spindle, you will need to draft smoothly and steadily to keep the spindle from swinging back and forth, although swaying is not a great concern unless it becomes extreme.

Second worsted-method opinion
The other school of thought proclaims that you must draw the fibers *away* from the spindle (with

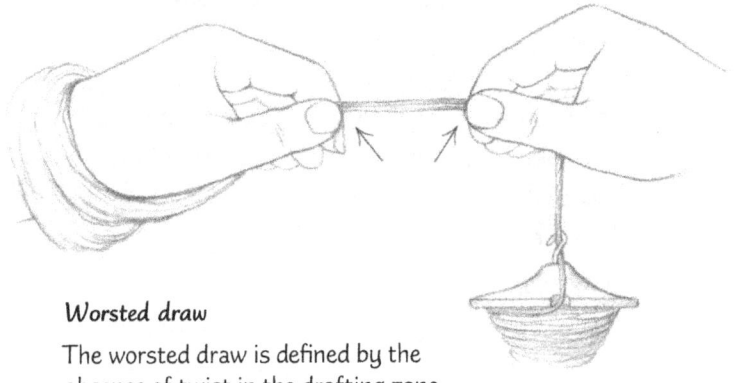

Worsted draw
The worsted draw is defined by the absence of twist in the drafting zone.

the second hand), then allow the twist to enter while advancing the yarn toward the spindle, smoothing the fibers as in the previous method.

In this technique, it's easy to extend the drafting zone too far, so that the yarn gets thinner than you want it to be. There is no quick remedy for this problem; you must break off and then rejoin the fiber supply.

So who's right?
In my opinion, the method to use is a personal choice. I can work either way and produce the same results—any difference in my yarns is not discernible. I have seen spinners produce wonderful worsted yarns using a hybrid of the two techniques. The choice is not about right or wrong, but about what works for you.

My preference? I usually work with the first method, drawing out the fibers with the hand that controls the twist.

In either case, the idea is to draft yarn equal to about half a fiber's length while keeping the twist out of the drafting zone—say, draft about 1½ inches (3.8 cm) if your fibers are 3 inches (7.6 cm) long. (This is why worsted spinning is called "short draw.") Then smooth down the fibers between your fingers as you allow the twist to enter the drafted fibers.

Worsted draw from the fold
There's one other alternative for worsted spinning, called a worsted draw from the fold.

Spinning technique

Either spin from a lock of combed fiber or pull off a section of top that is about the length of the longest fibers—a 3-inch (7.5-cm) section when the fibers are about that length. Fold the section over your forefinger and spin with a worsted technique, drafting the fibers off the edge of the fold. Some spinners prefer to fold the fiber over a finger (usually the forefinger); others hold the folded fibers between the thumb and forefinger.

This is an easy method of spinning worsted. It offers good control, but does not permit the long fiber supply that I like; you need to keep joining in new short sections of folded fibers

Also, your yarn will be highly directional: because the fiber ends all lie in the same way, they will all protrude from the yarn in one direction. This is great for embroidery yarns! Thread a spun-from-the-fold yarn into your needle so that the ends are smoothed back with each stitch.

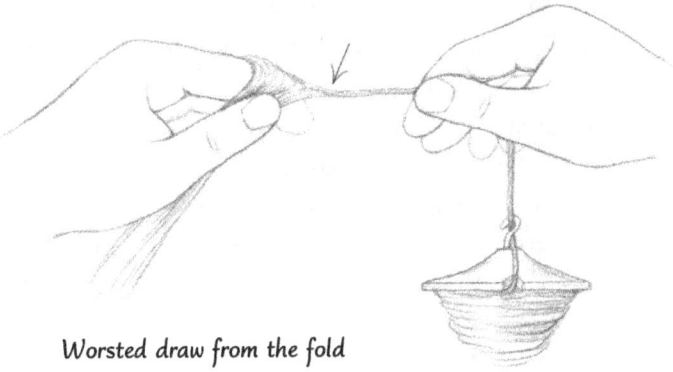

Worsted draw from the fold
Fold a lock of combed fiber or top and spin from the point of the fold.

Spinning in the Old Way

Twist and diameter

Controlling twist and diameter is often a topic of conversation among handspinners, especially those who use spinning wheels. In some cases, the spinner who wants to maintain consistency carefully counts the number of treadles required for one complete revolution of the wheel, and measures the length of the draw in relation to a specific number of revolutions. This kind of gauging is not appropriate in high-whorling.

The simple approach

The principles involved can be simply stated: Diameter is determined by the number of fibers allowed to remain in the drafting zone. Twist is determined by the number of rotations allowed to hold the fibers together.

Measuring diameter and twist

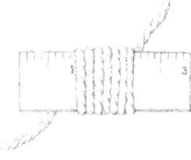

Diameter, as described in chapter 2, can be measured by the number of times a yarn will wrap around a given measure on a ruler, referred to as *wraps per inch* (w.p.i.; see page 47).

Twist is specified in *twists per inch*, but this is difficult to measure. Instead, most spinners judge the amount of twist in their yarns by relying on a visual means to judge the amount of twist called *angle of twist*. The less twist in the yarn, the steeper the angle of twist. The more twist in the yarn, the shallower the angle of twist.

Spinning technique

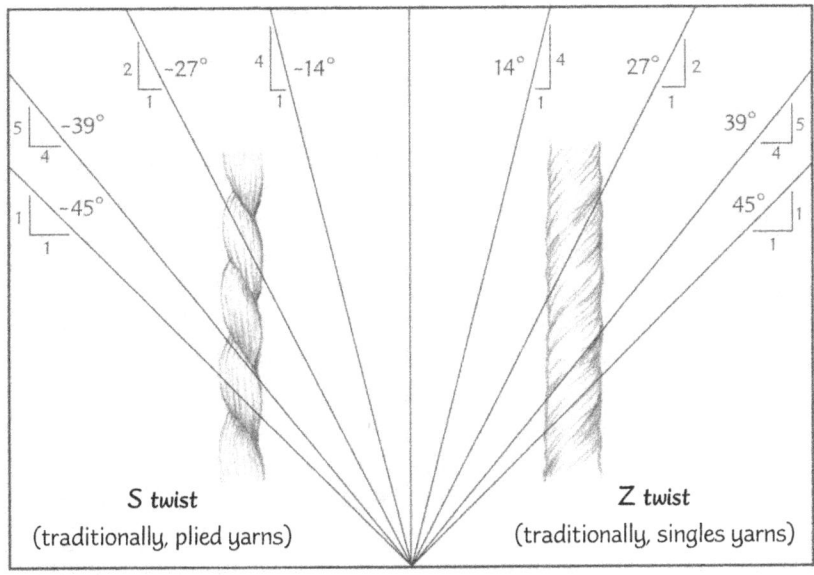

Twist gauge: How much twist is in your yarn?

A twist gauge consists of angular rays of both positive and negative angles. The negative rays measure S twists and the positive rays measure Z twists.

You may obtain a commercially manufactured gauge or you can construct one yourself with a protractor. A twist gauge will contain a measured sequence of intervals from 0 degrees (straight up) to 90 and -90 degrees (the horizontal line at the bottom).

Twist angles for popular weights of yarn correspond to slope ratios of 1:1, 5:4, 2:1, and 4:1. These sample angles are shown in the illustration.

You can check your yarn for consistency in twist amounts by laying the yarn over the gauge and aligning the twist angle to the angle of the gauge. In the samples shown here, the singles yarn (on the right) is spun at 39 degrees and the plied yarn (on the left) at 27 degrees.

Spinning in the Old Way

Spinning consistent yarn

Consistency of twist and diameter is another matter. Spinning yard after yard, skein after skein, takes practice. Many spinners judge their consistency by allowing a section of yarn to ply back on itself, making it possible to evaluate both diameter and angle of twist more readily. But if you simply relax the yarn to let it ply back on itself, you will not have a representative sample. First, you need to perform this check with freshly spun yarn. Second, the ply-back inserts itself in the parts of the yarn where there is the most twist—in its thinnest portions.

How to prepare a yarn sample

1. To get a good sample, spin about 20 to 24 inches (50 to 60 cm) of yarn. Hold it so it is tensioned by

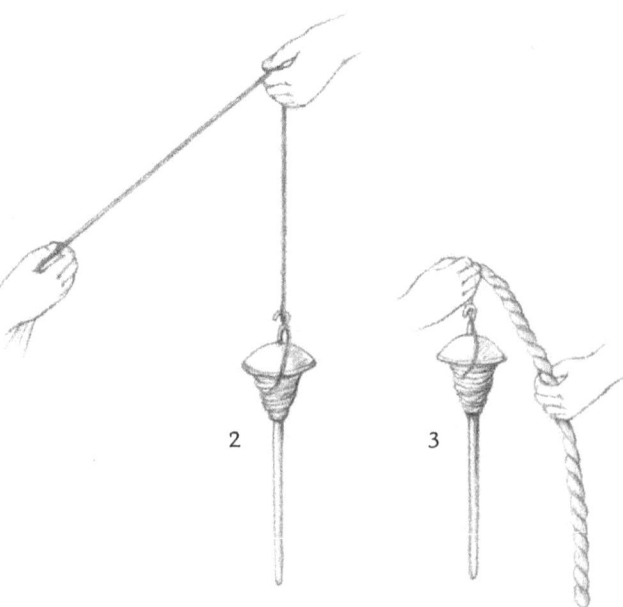

Spinning technique

the weight of the spindle. This yarn needs to be freshly spun.

2. With your free hand, grasp this length of yarn in its middle.

3. Fold the length until the two segments are parallel and right next to each other. Hold the two ends together with your spindle hand. Release the tension and let the twist wrap the strands around each other while you run the fingers of your free hand toward the fold. Smooth the sample several times with your hand, moving from the spindle end to the fold end.

This will give you a representative sample of that section. You may then examine this sample using a twist gauge like the one illustrated on page 119.

Using a sample card

Since I cannot trust my memory, for each project I make a sample card that I use to judge my consistency. I use a piece of mat board about 4 by 6 inches (10 by 15 cm). Scraps of mat board are readily available in the wastebaskets at framing shops. I use colored mat board for white yarn, and white for colored yarn. I cut one short slit near the lower right corner of the longer side, and another slit near the upper left corner.

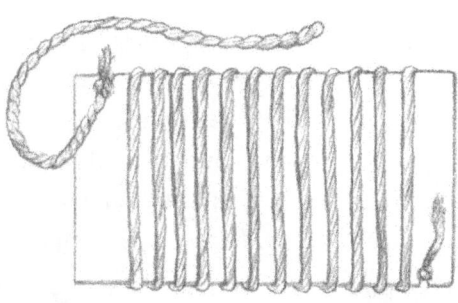

Sample card

This simple visual guide to consistency will improve your ability to spin an even yarn.

Spinning in the Old Way

I take about a 3-yard (2.75-m) length of singles yarn that I want to match, make a rolled knot at one end, then secure that end of the yarn in the first slit. The sample must be made of newly spun yarn because the twist forces will be altered if the yarn is allowed to rest while wound under tension, as it is on the spindle shaft. I wrap this yarn around and around the card until I come to the second slit, with the goal of having a 20- to 24-inch (50- to 60-cm) section of the yarn still available beyond the slit. I ply this back on itself, as described on pages 120 and 121.

Notes on the sample card

My sample card is now suitable for reference as I spin. It shows me what the singles should look like and how a plied-back sample should appear. For reference, in case I lay my work aside for a while and forget what techniques were involved, I note on the card the fiber's identity, along with the preparation and spinning techniques used.

It's not done until it's finished!

An important point to consider is that yarn can change in the finishing process—when it is washed and possibly blocked. Woolen yarns can alter dramatically, becoming shorter and more lofty. Worsted yarns do not change as much.

Before spinning a lot, finish your sample

Nonetheless, to be sure you will get the results you want, spin a small sample skein and carry it through the finishing processes described in the next chapter.

Spinning technique

Joining

Sooner or later your fiber supply will come to an end. To continue spinning, you must now attach a new fiber supply.

There is no big mystery to joining, just common sense. If you spin all the fibers in the depleting fiber supply, you must lay the new fiber supply over twisted yarn to continue spinning. This leads to a weak join that can actually slip off the newly spun yarn. Instead, stop spinning when a small portion of the depleting fiber supply remains unspun. Fan out the fibers in this tail and fan out one end of the new fiber supply. Lay these two fanned-out portions over each other. The overlapping area should contain about the same amount of fiber that you have been working with. Draft the two as a single unit that looks just like the surrounding yarn. This will make a smooth, sturdy join because the fibers from both ends are fully integrated.

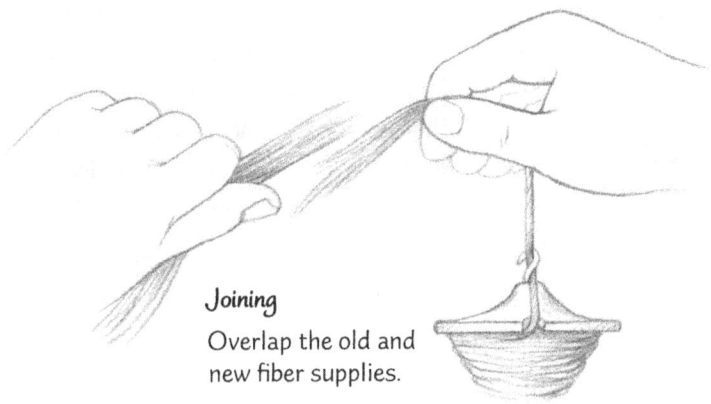

Joining
Overlap the old and new fiber supplies.

What if the yarn breaks while you are spinning? This usually occurs when the fibers have thinned out. Too much twist rushes to the thin spot and breaks the fibers. The broken tail of yarn will contain a lot of twist. I recommend breaking off the yarn attached to the spindle above the highly twisted section—you can, if necessary, untwist a small segment of yarn so the twist no longer holds it together and pull the two ends to separate the pieces. In any case, remove any spun portion on the fiber-supply end. Give the tip of the yarn a backward roll between your fingers to remove twist from the yarn; fan out the fibers as much as possible. Then proceed with overlapping and spinning as for a normal join.

Fixing breaks during spinning

Not-quite-high-whorl spindles

Salish spindle

I was slow to realize that my big Salish Indian spindle is a type of high-whorl handspindle. Spindles of this type were used by native people in the Pacific Northwest to spin bulky, two-ply weaving yarns for blankets. After the introduction of knitting to this region by Europeans in the nineteenth century, the primary use of the spindles shifted to creating the soft, bulky, natural-colored wool singles used for knitting the Cowichan people's characteristic boldly designed sweaters.

Large spindles from the Pacific Northwest

Spinning technique

The traditional method
The method I learned for the use of the Salish spindle begins with thigh-spinning to make the initial yarn to attach to the spindle.

Begin the yarn by rolling the fibers downward on the left thigh with the left hand, while drafting up and away with the right hand. Wind the accumulating yarn in a figure eight around thumb and forefinger.

When you have a sufficient length of yarn, fold the figure-eight shaped yarn with the end in the center, somewhat like a bird's nest (pages 82–83). As you wind on, draw the yarn out of the folded figure-eight shape and wind it around the shaft clockwise, as tightly as possible. Spiral the last portion up to the top of the spindle and begin spinning, rolling the spindle up on the right thigh.

The spindle should rest on the thigh at about a 45-degree angle when spinning. Otherwise the yarn will either slide off the tip of the spindle or inappropriately wrap around its shaft.

1. Roll the spindle up your leg as you draw out the roving. The length of just-spun yarn between the spindle tip and your hand will pop off the end of the spindle once for every full rotation. Continue to roll the spindle and draft fiber until your arm is fully extended.

Spinning in the Old Way

2

2. Turn the spindle so it is upright. Unwind the yarn that is spiraling up the shaft by pulling the new yarn away from the spindle (this is a counterclockwise movement). Wind the yarn onto the spindle, to form a cop, by turning the spindle clockwise. As you finish winding, spiral the last bit of yarn up to the spindle tip so you are ready to spin again.

My adaptations

I have departed from tradition by adding a large hook to the tip of my spindle. This keeps the yarn from popping off the tip as I spin, so my movements are smoother and there is less stress on the yarn as it is being spun.

In addition, I can now begin my yarn the same way that I do for my other high-whorl spindles, attaching the fibers directly to the hook when spinning the initial section. When I spin, I do not need to worry about the angle of the spindle because the twist will go directly into the yarn. With a hook installed, drafting ahead of the advancing twist works as well as attenuating.

Akha spindle

For my finest spinning, I prefer to use a little Akha handspindle from Southeast Asia. The tiny Akha

Spinning technique

spindles weigh about 8 grams (1/3 ounce)—sometimes even less. The Akha spindle was designed to be used as a hand-supported spindle with cotton fibers. I find mine is also delightful to use as a high-whorl spindle.

Tiny spindles from Southeast Asia

Traditional method

Traditionally, the spindle is twirled within the curl of the fingers. Drafting and inserting twist are two separate steps.

1. Turn the spindle by flicking the thumb against the forefinger to build up twist. The rotating spindle is supported by the three other fingers.

2. To extend the yarn, draft the fibers and let the twist run into them.

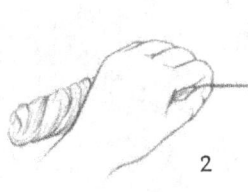

My adaptation

I use the Akha as a classic high-whorl spindle to make incredibly fine yarns. I rotate the shaft on my leg. The only difference from a regular high-whorl spindle is in the winding on: because the cop develops above the whorl, you must spiral the yarn up the shaft before catching it in the carved hook at the tip.

THE MOST BEAUTIFUL WORK WILL BE COMPLETED WHEN THE ARTIST ENTIRELY ABSORBS HIMSELF AND HIS HONOR IN HIS WORK.

Soetsu Yanagi, *The Unknown Craftsman*

6

Singles, plies, and cables
Many different yarns, from simple to complex

Being able to make one strand of yarn is only the beginning, although you can use a single strand directly and this chapter will explain how.

Many times you will want to spin two or more strands together, uniting them in a *plied yarn*. The most common handspun knitting yarns consist of two single strands spun Z and plied together S to produce what is called a *balanced yarn*.

Plied yarns can be re-combined. Each plying step most often involves reversing the twist direction of the previous step. If singles are spun clockwise, they are plied counterclockwise. The next step, if there is one, usually goes clockwise again.

Every time you spin or ply yarn, you change the amount and type of twist in it. Spinning is all about managing twist: the directions and the amounts.

The first half of this chapter considers the theory of twist in singles and in the workhorse plied

Spinning is all about managing twist

yarns, plus a personal favorite: the cabled yarn. The second half of the chapter covers the practical aspects of plying with a high-whorl spindle.

Twist = energy

Twist is a form of energy that you generate by rotating the spindle. The energy gets transferred into the fibers, holding them together to form yarn. Spindles slow down and stop rotating when all the energy has been transferred to the yarn.

Unstable and stable yarns

Yarns are either *unstable* or *stable*. Unless the twist is stabilized within a yarn, the energy wants to escape from the fibers—to untwist them. This is why your spindle starts to rotate backward after the energy has been transferred to the yarn.

You can temporarily keep twist from escaping by putting tension on both ends of the strand. Yarn temporarily becomes more stable when it sits on a spindle shaft or in a ball for a long time.

You can more permanently set twist by finishing the yarn (my favorite method is described in chapter 7). You can also stabilize twist by plying singles together in a way that makes the twist balanced. This is the most important type of plying to understand. You will use it constantly,

Balanced ply
In this single strand of plied yarn, the plying twist balances the twist in the singles. Note that the apparent angle of twist in the singles now runs parallel to the length of yarn.

Singles, plies, and cables

especially, but of course not only, if you are making yarns for knitting. (The theory of plying will be along in a few pages.)

Active and relaxed (or balanced) twist

Unstable yarn moves because it contains *active* twist. When you knit a rectangular swatch from unstable

How active twist amounts affect skeined yarn

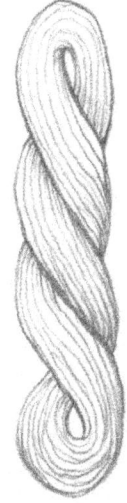

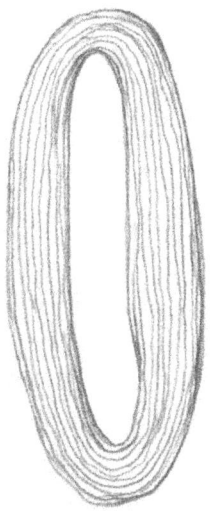

Active S twist

Yarn with active S twist plies back on itself and shows a Z-twist orientation in the skein.

Singles spun S and not set OR two-ply made from Z-spun singles plied with too much S (overplied).

Active Z twist

Yarn with active Z twist plies back on itself and shows an S-twist orientation in the skein.

Singles spun Z and not set OR two-ply made from Z-spun singles plied with not enough S (underplied).

Balanced twist

Yarn with balanced twist hangs in a relaxed, open loop.

Two-ply yarn made from Z-spun singles plied with a balancing amount of S twist.

Spinning in the Old Way

Z-twist singles

Active Z twist in knitting

If you knit with active-twist yarn, the finished fabric will be distorted by a bias slant, as shown in this stockinette "rectangle."

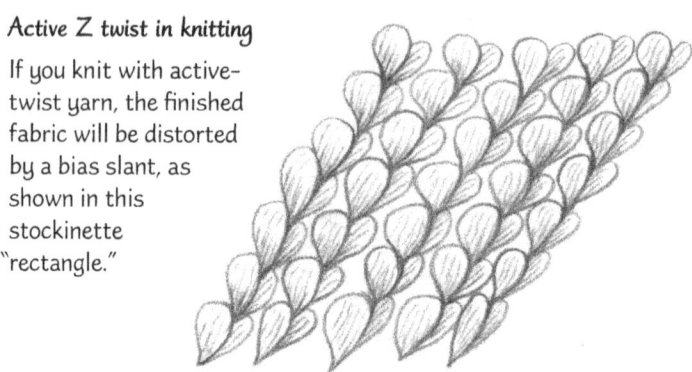

yarn, the swatch distorts. The angles at its corners skew in one direction or another, creating a bias slant. Which way they skew depends on the direction of the active twist. This effect can be prevented by neutralizing the twist in the yarn.

Stable yarn stays put because it contains *relaxed* twist (either balanced or successfully set): it does not move around. A rectangular swatch knitted from stable yarn has right-angled corners.

As long as there is not too much active twist, you can knit with active-twist yarn although you will need to sternly block the fabric into shape every time you wash it. With an excess of active twist, even blocking will not be enough to tame the distortion.

Singles

Turning loose fibers into a strand of yarn produces singles yarn (sometimes mistakenly called *one-ply*... there's no ply to it at all!). A singles yarn is

Singles, plies, and cables

unstable and tends to twist back on itself. Hold a freshly spun singles under tension, then relax your hands. The center of the strand curls around itself.

Using singles

Does this mean that we cannot use singles? No, of course not! Singles have been used successfully for as long as textiles have been around. It does mean that we need to learn how to use them. During the 1960s and 1970s, many handspinners were unaware of the problem active twist can create in knitted fabric. As a result, singles gained a bad reputation that they do not deserve.

Singles can be used in weaving, as long as they are strong enough, which means that they contain enough twist to hold together while they are being woven. Warp yarns are the vertical strands through which the weft yarns (horizontal strands) are woven. Singles can be used as warp or weft, although warp yarns need to be stronger than weft yarns. For those who are interested in exploring the use of singles in weaving, highly twisted singles with active twist forces can be used to create interesting woven textures.

Singles can be used for weaving

I like to use singles in both my knitting and my tapestry weaving. There is a long history of the use of singles in knitting, including the tradition of bulky Cowichan sweaters from North America and the much older traditions preserved in Eastern European socks. Singles in what we would call

Singles can be used for knitting

133

sportweight are favored in parts of Turkey, while combining singles without benefit of plying—simply holding the strands together during knitting—is common throughout Eastern Europe.

Twist levels in singles

If the amount of twist in the singles is moderate, you can effectively set the twist by finishing the yarn. Finishing involves applying heat and moisture, and my favorite finishing method is described in chapter 7. The amount of twist that can be neutralized through finishing depends on the size of the yarn in relation to the characteristics of the fibers (fineness, length, and waviness; the last of these is also called *crimp*).

The information I offer here will give you guidelines for developing what becomes an instinctive awareness of how much twist you can work successfully with in singles. For knitting, you can safely spin:

Wool type	Singles yarn type	Wraps per inch (2.5 cm)	Twist angles
medium or long	bulky	4 to 8	14–21 degrees
fine, medium, or long	heavy	10 to 12	21–30 degrees
fine or medium	medium	14 to 16	30–39 degrees

Singles, plies, and cables

As a general rule, the finer the yarn, the more twist you can use before you see the effects in a fabric.

In addition, it's been my experience that the finer the crimp, or waviness, in the fiber, the more readily the twist energy can be neutralized. When I spin bulky singles, I use medium wool with tight crimp even though the fibers are short in comparison to the long wools. It is tempting to use those lovely long wools to make softly spun singles yarns because less twist is required to secure the fibers within the yarn. Yet the open, wavy crimp in the long wools produces a dense yarn in which it's more difficult to neutralize the twist.

Wool choice and twist level

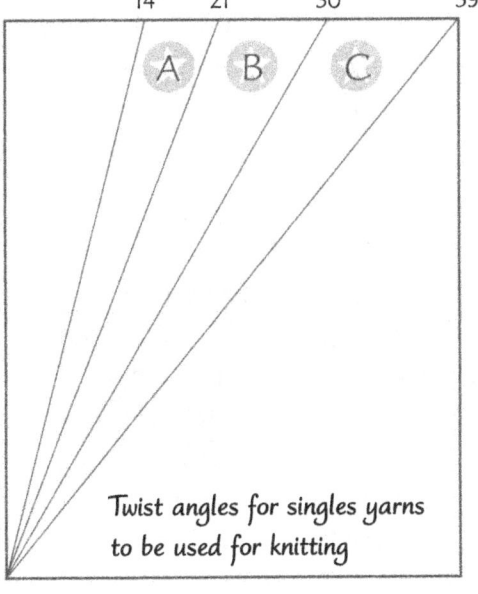

Twist angles for singles yarns to be used for knitting

Bulky yarn
A — 4–8 wraps per inch (2.5 cm), medium and long wools, 14 to 21°

Heavyweight yarn
B — 10–12 wraps per inch (2.5 cm), fine, medium, and long wools, 21 to 30°

Medium-weight yarn
C — 14–16 wraps per inch (2.5 cm), fine and medium wools, 30 to 39°

135

Spinning in the Old Way

Furrows in knitted fabric

Neutralized Z twist

Even when the twist has been set in a high-twist singles, knitted stockinette fabric develops furrows. With dominant Z twist, the left side of each stitch is wider than the right side.

Z-twist singles

At higher levels of twist, the surface of a fabric knitted with singles develops furrows even if the yarn has been finished. One half of each knit stitch appears fat and wide; the twist lines in this half-stitch are approximately vertical. The other half of each stitch is skinny. The difference between the halves of the stitches results in a fabric with distinct vertical ridges. The more twist in the yarn, the deeper the furrow.

Plied yarns

Two, three, four, or more singles yarns can be combined to make a final yarn. For handspun used in knitting, two- and three-ply yarns are most common. Two-ply yarns appear frequently in older ethnic pieces.

I prefer two-ply yarns because they seem to result in fabric with a robust, energetic hand (feel)

Singles, plies, and cables

and appearance. Three-ply yarns are more softly rounded, with an enhanced propensity to drape nicely. They are great for cowl-neck garments and for shawls. I think that four-ply yarns are bland and somewhat lifeless (though very durable) and that spinning five-ply yarns is masochistic.

How many plies?

Since singles can be used, why bother with plying? In general, more plies mean greater final strength and durability in the yarn. For a given weight of yarn, the plied version will contain more twist than the singles. Greater twist contains more fiber ends and thus reduces pilling, enhances abrasion-resistance, and generally increases strength (up to a point—excessive twist makes yarn brittle).

Why ply?

Balanced twist

A yarn that has been plied so the plying twist neutralizes the twist in the singles is called *balanced* and it can be used anywhere.

Here is where we come to the importance of reversing the twist direction. If you ply singles in the same direction in which you originally spun them, you add more twist of the same type. The yarn becomes unruly and harsh.

Why spin in one direction and ply in the other?

On the other hand, when you ply two identical singles in the reverse twist direction, the tendency of the active twist in each strand to untwist, encouraged by the plying, wraps the two singles around each other and makes an integrated two-ply yarn. The result is, ideally, a balanced yarn.

Spinning in the Old Way

The yarn itself will show you how much plying twist to use

You need a certain amount of plying twist to accomplish this. For every pair of identical singles, a specific amount of plying twist will produce a balanced two-ply. Although measures of twist angles can help us understand the principles at work here, there are so many variables involved that the best answer to "What is the right amount of plying twist to make a relaxed yarn?" comes from the yarn itself.

How much plying twist is enough?

To determine how much plying twist is needed to make a balanced two-ply yarn, prepare a freshly spun sample as described on page 120. When a newly spun length of singles plies back on itself, the resulting two-ply will be balanced.

Make a sample card (page 121) and use it as a standard against which to visually compare your yarn from time to time as you ply. As long as your singles contain the same amount of twist as the original singles and your plied yarn looks like what is on the sample, your two-ply will be balanced.

The process for checking twist levels in yarns with more than two plies is not as direct as the ply-back technique, but the results should be similar. For more complex yarns, you also spin fresh singles and make a sample of the finished yarn that you intend to produce. The sample should be relaxed.

How NOT to check for a balanced twist amount

Many spinners will tell you to begin to ply your singles and then check a length of the newly plied yarn

Singles, plies, and cables

by holding it so it hangs in a low curve, like a jump rope. They say that if the yarn hangs in a straight, relaxed loop and does not attempt to twist back on itself at all, it is balanced. But that is only the case if the singles have been freshly spun.

If the singles yarns have been stored for a while—for example, on a handspindle or in a ball—the twist is likely to have been temporarily set. The longer the singles have been stored and the higher the temperature and humidity, the more temporary setting will have occurred.

Common method of checking twist amounts doesn't work

The resulting plied yarn will appear relaxed even though it does not contain enough plying twist. It will be *underplied*. A truly balanced yarn spun from temporarily set singles will not appear to be relaxed when you test it this way. It will seem to have too much plying twist.

Cabled yarns

Cabling is a process of plying together yarns that have already been plied—for example, taking two two-ply yarns and plying them together to make a four-ply yarn. This is not at all the same as a yarn made from four singles all plied together at once.

Ply, and ply again

For cabled yarns, you must spin the singles in one direction, ply in the opposite direction, and ply again (cable) in the first direction. As in the previous cases, the goal is a balanced yarn. The process is obviously somewhat more complicated.

Spinning in the Old Way

Why bother?

Why would you go to this much effort? Possibly you would want to compensate for reduced strength and/or durability in the fiber. For instance, a fine, soft wool like Merino does not make a good sock yarn as a singles or a two-ply. It doesn't wear well at all. Yet it would be so comfortable to feel that warm, gentle fiber on your feet! If you spin worsted singles, ply them together, and then cable, Merino can make an incredibly soft yarn that is sufficiently durable for socks. Cabling also makes a visually lovely yarn.

To make a balanced cable, you must begin with *unbalanced plies*: the two-plies that you use must have "too much" plying twist in them (they must be *overplied*). Then these two-plies are cabled (again in the opposite direction from that in which the plies were created) to produce the final balanced yarn.

On page 156 I describe the technical details of managing these steps.

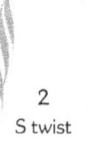

1
Z twist

2
S twist

3
Z twist

Cable construction

The formula for a four-ply cable is this:

Step 1. 4 singles, Z-twisted

Step 2. ⇨ 2 two-plies, S-twisted and overplied

Step 3. ⇨ 1 four-ply, Z-twisted (cabled) to produce a balanced yarn

Singles, plies, and cables

Further notes on plying

Your plying will not be perfect. It does not need to be perfect! As long as your twist amounts are in approximately the right ranges, the finishing process discussed in the next chapter will neutralize any residual twist energy.

Perfection is not required

My discussion of cabling only introduces a whole realm of spinning known as *yarn design*. Because I knit and weave in ways that work best with well-constructed, simple yarns, the information in this chapter emphasizes the skills required to spin those yarns. If you would like to make novelty yarns, rest assured that you can do so with your high-whorl spindle. Either consult a guide to yarn design intended for wheel-spinners and adapt the instructions or just experiment on your own.

Yarn design

The how-to of plying

Plying on a handspindle is seldom discussed. I have often wondered why, and finally came to the conclusion that most spinners today have not found a comfortable way to ply their handspindle-spun yarn. I was determined to find a way that would work for me, one that (1) would give me good control over the tension on the strands so that my yarn would be evenly plied, (2) would only require simple, portable tools, and (3) could be done anywhere.

Yes, you can ply well on a spindle

I found two!

Spinning in the Old Way

Common inefficient methods

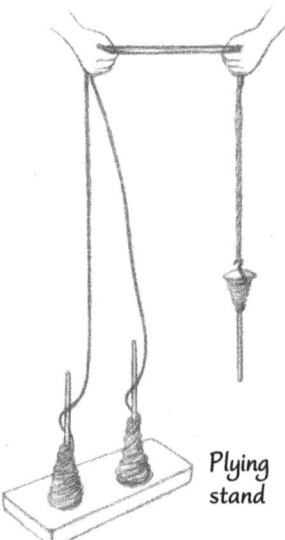

Plying stand

I'm also going to introduce you to the methods I tried that I consider less satisfactory. Some are better than others, and you may find yourself in a situation where one of these techniques is just what you need.

And then I will explain methods that work well for me and I will show you how to use them both separately and in combination with each other.

Less-satisfactory plying techniques

Cops and balls on stands or in bowls
Three closely related techniques do not incorporate any means of tensioning the yarn, so I end up with tangles. One involves cops that have

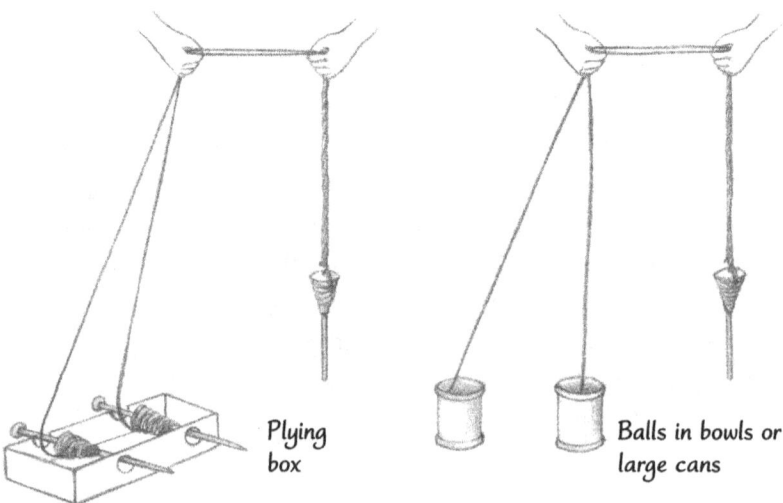

Plying box

Balls in bowls or large cans

Singles, plies, and cables

been transferred to a stand. In the second, a box with holes in its sides supports horizontal rods to which the cops have been transferred. In the third, the singles are rolled into balls and set in bowls or large cans. In my opinion, the results are dismal.

Better plying techniques

The overhead ring

The fourth method, although similar, is serviceable, although it is not nomadic enough for me. You need a ceiling with a ring or a hook set into it. This technique was common in diverse cultures located as far apart as Eastern Europe and the northwest coast of North America, where it was used by the Coast Salish people.

It involves placing the singles on the ground, threading them through an overhead ring, and attaching the ends to the spindle. This set-up places the singles under enough tension to facilitate even plying.

Peruvian hand-wrap plying

Peruvian hand-wrap plying is relatively tangle-free and portable. It's intended for making two-ply yarns where both plies are the same (you work from both ends of the same strand), and is only suited to plying small amounts of yarn.

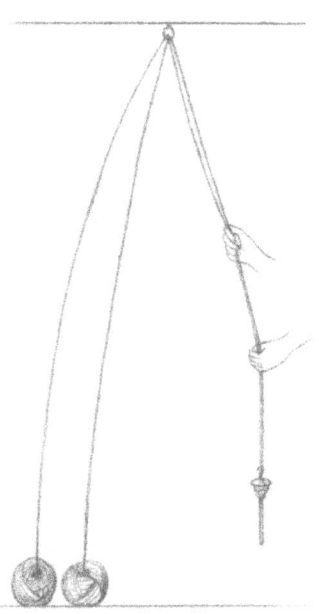

Overhead tension ring

Less common, better methods

Spinning in the Old Way

It begins with wrapping the yarn around the wrist as well as through a crossover on the big finger. You unwind the yarn directly from the spindle onto your hand and then ply from the two ends toward the center of the single strand. I find unwinding from the spindle in this way awkward with all but the smaller spindles, so I invert the spindle between my feet, then draw the yarn up and off the spindle while I wind (see page 148 for the setup).

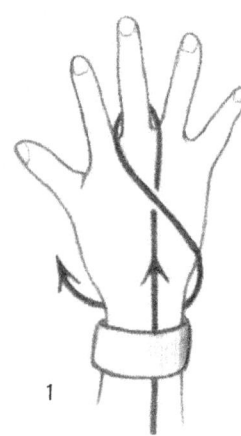

The procedure is not complicated. Secure the yarn end to keep it out of the way, using the same method you use to secure roving when you spin singles. I tuck the end under my bracelet. Although traditionally the yarn is wrapped around the left hand, I make the wrapping on my right hand and control the spindle with my left. During plying, the yarn will stay on the hand where you have wrapped it, so the decision you make when you start is the decision you stay with throughout the process. (Yes, you can carefully shift the wrapped yarn to the other hand if you begin working and discover it would be much easier for you to be using the opposite hands.)

To do the wrapping, it may be easier to follow the illustrations than the written description! But I will give you both pictures and words.

Singles, plies, and cables

1. Take the yarn up the back of your hand and around your big finger from right to left. Then bring it down, cross it over the beginning yarn, and take it around the front of the wrist from the little-finger side to the thumb side.

2. Bring the yarn up the back of the hand again, encircle the big finger from left to right, and take it down and around the front of the wrist from the thumb side to the little-finger side. You will have an X crossover at the knuckle of your big finger, with one angular strand at each side extending to your wrist.

3. Continue to wrap, alternating steps 1 and 2, until all the yarn has been transferred. The yarn never passes over the palm of your hand. It only goes over the back of the hand, around the big finger, and across the front of the wrist. 3a shows how the wrapping looks on the palm of your hand and 3b shows how it looks on the back of your hand. Wrap loosely; as the strands build up, the tension will tighten.

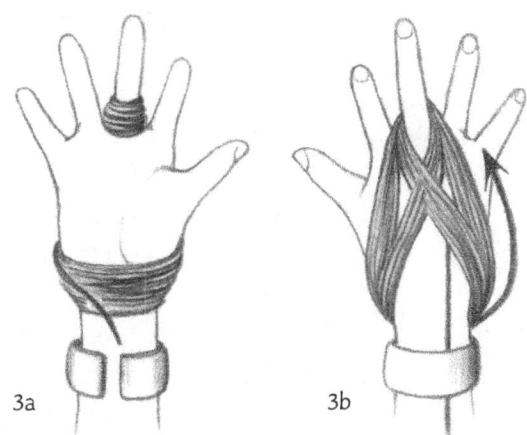

3a Wrapping seen from palm side

3b Wrapping seen from back of hand

Spinning in the Old Way

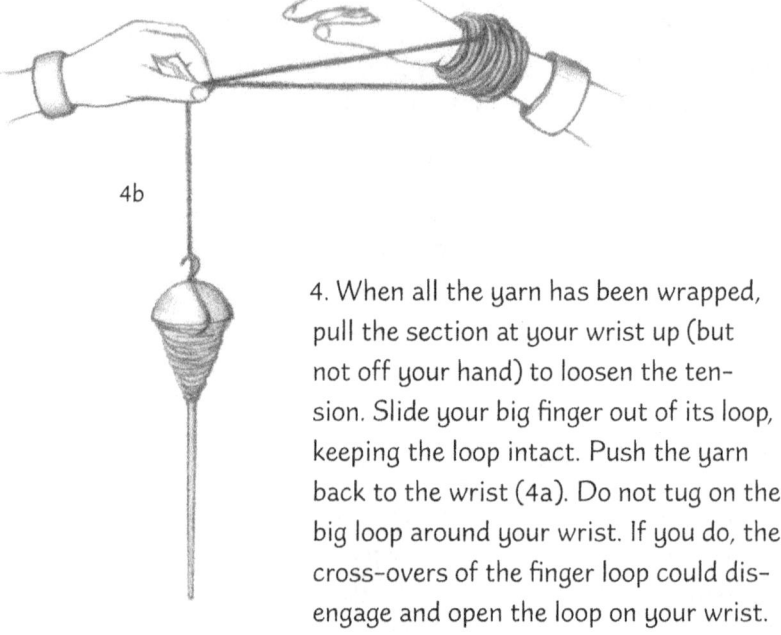

4a

4b

4. When all the yarn has been wrapped, pull the section at your wrist up (but not off your hand) to loosen the tension. Slide your big finger out of its loop, keeping the loop intact. Push the yarn back to the wrist (4a). Do not tug on the big loop around your wrist. If you do, the cross-overs of the finger loop could disengage and open the loop on your wrist. The loops are held together only by a bit of friction. You are now ready to make your two-ply yarn from the two ends (4b).

Other traditional plying techniques

When I delved into nomadic techniques of the Middle East and Central Asia, I found to my dismay that nomadic people often stored singles while moving around and did not ply them until they established living quarters where they would stay for a while. Then the women would gather communally and would work with a small, crude plying wheel, one that could be easily dismantled for transport. Two or three women would hold the singles strands

Community plying

Singles, plies, and cables

After all my research and trials, *I still faced the problem of* **how to ply with total mobility.** *A version of the center-pull ball led me to the first* **elegant** *solution.*

while another turned the wheel to ply the yarn. This is a nice idea, but I am a solitary spinner.

I came across another discovery when I was studying the ethnic socks of this same region: in many cases, multiple strands were simply held together and were not plied at all. I am not fond of this idea because I find it harder to maintain an even tension when knitting with multiple, unplied strands.

Doubling instead of plying

After all my research and trials, I still faced the problem of how to ply with total mobility. Especially when making samples, today's spinners often ply from two ends of a center-pull ball. I have never been fond of this technique because I end up with a snarl about two-thirds of the way through. The active twist in the singles is the culprit; when it tries to relax, I am left with a mess no matter how I hold the ball.

Center-pull ball

Favorite plying technique #1:
Off the nostepinne

Yet a version of the center-pull ball technique led me to an elegant plying solution.

It occurred to me that I wind my knitting yarn into a center-pull ball with a nostepinne—why not ply from the nostepinne, keeping it in place throughout the process?

This worked. Keeping the nostepinne at the center of the ball tamed the snarling produced by the active twist in the singles. I could also push the ball onto the wider part of the nostepinne to secure it when I had to put my work down temporarily.

Plying off both ends of the ball has advantages beyond that of mobility. Many novice high-whorlers tend to spin finer at the beginning of a spindle full of yarn and thicker later on, when the weight of the spindle has increased. When they ply off both ends of a single ball, they end up with a more consistent yarn: the early thin section matches up with the later thick one. There are also no leftovers at the end of plying, because one continuous length is being plied toward its middle.

Removing yarn from the high-whorl spindle

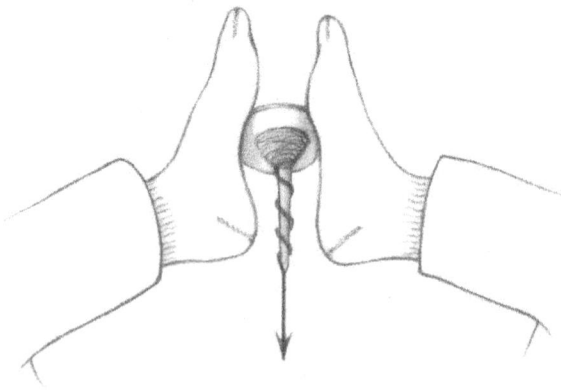

Technique 1: Feet

When the spindle is inverted (whorl down) and held between your feet, the yarn will wind off around the shaft and you can wind it onto the nostepinne.

Singles, plies, and cables

Supporting the spindle so you can wind off the yarn
The first thing to do is to get the yarn off the spindle and onto the nostepinne. I found two simple techniques for managing the spindle during this process that work for most spinners.

You can turn the spindle upside down and place it between your feet. I hold the spindle steady by turning my feet on their sides and securing the spindle between my arches. I lean the spindle shaft slightly toward my body and the yarn winds readily off the tip of the shaft.

Alternately, you can use a plastic tube to support the shaft of the spindle as you wind the yarn off. You will need to be creative in locating this supplementary tool, which should be both small and lightweight enough not to overload your collection of equipment.

One type of long, skinny tube is used on the stems of single flowers to keep them fresh; a standard size is 11 cm (about 4½ inches) long and

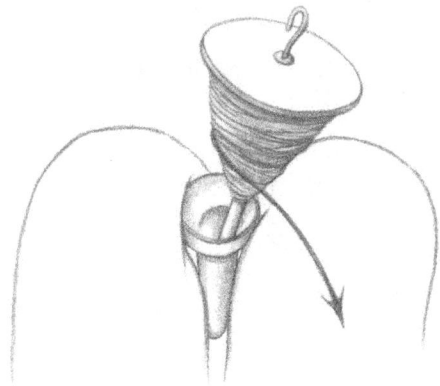

Technique 2: Knees
Brace a container for the spindle shaft between your knees. I use a large outer cylinder from a veterinary syringe. The shaft of the spindle rotates freely within the container while you wind the yarn onto the nostepinne.

Spinning in the Old Way

will fit small spindles. Remove the rubber gasket at the top that keeps the water inside and you will have the narrow cylinder that you need. Veterinarians use syringes of several sizes; the outer plastic cylinder of a syringe will meet your needs. Once you have the concept in mind, you may find other sources for a container of the appropriate size and shape. Some cigars come in plastic tubes. You want a relatively soft material that will not mar your spindle, like plastic instead of metal.

Once you have located a plastic cylinder, turn it so the opening (or larger opening) is up. Hold it between your knees, and insert the shaft of your spindle. The handspindle will turn freely within the tube as you wind off the yarn.

How to wind yarn onto a nostepinne

If you have never worked with a nostepinne, how to use it can be a mystery. After all, it is just a tapered stick with a groove cut around the narrower end.

This narrow end is the top. The wider portion at the base is what you hold as you turn it.

1. You can use either hand to hold the nostepinne. With the other hand, wrap the end of the yarn around the groove at the top several times. For the yarn to be snugly held in place, tuck the very end of the yarn under the wraps.

2. When the end of the yarn has been secured, spiral the yarn partway down the nostepinne to a wider spot on its shaft.

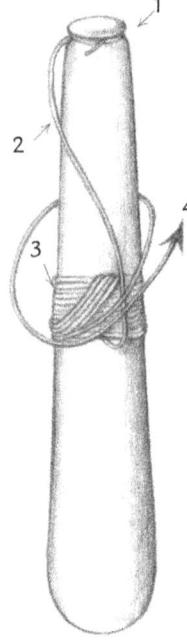

Winding yarn onto a nostepinne

1 Secure end
2 Spiral down
3 Wrap core
4 Wrap at 45° angle

Singles, plies, and cables

3. With the thumb of the hand that is holding the nostepinne, hold this yarn in place. To secure the yarn here, take several wraps around the circumference of the nostepinne, going straight around the shaft. This will both hold the yarn in place and begin to build a small core for the center-pull ball that will be your end result.

4. For the remainder of the wrapping, hold the yarn at a 45-degree angle, rotating the nostepinne as you wrap over the core so that the ball builds up evenly around the tool. After you have made several wraps, turn the nostepinne slightly to advance the wrapping to a new section—or simply rotate slowly and constantly as you wrap. Continue in this manner, wrapping and rotating, until all the yarn has been transferred to the nostepinne.

Leave the yarn on the nostepinne!

Don't take the ball off the nostepinne

Making a two-ply yarn

You are now ready to make a two-ply yarn. You will have two ends of yarn, one on the outside of the ball that you just wound onto the nostepinne and one that you will retrieve from the yarn that you wrapped into the groove when you began.

Tie these two ends together with an overhand knot. Slip the hook of the spindle through the space between the two strands that is formed by the knot.

Spinning in the Old Way

How to ply directly from a nostepinne

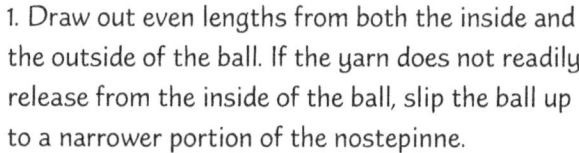

1. Draw out even lengths from both the inside and the outside of the ball. If the yarn does not readily release from the inside of the ball, slip the ball up to a narrower portion of the nostepinne.

2. Roll the handspindle in the opposite direction from that of spinning the singles. For singles, I control the spindle with my right hand, rolling up my right thigh. For plying, I reverse the process, holding the handspindle with my left hand, rolling up my left thigh.

Plying does not require as much twist as spinning singles does, so one vigorous, controlled roll of the shaft will ply a considerable length of yarn.

I am lucky to have a balcony adjacent to my studio from which I can ply a great length, then loop the yarn temporarily around my elbow and the tip of the nostepinne before I wind it onto the shaft of the handspindle. (I cannot spin singles in this manner because there is no way to continue rotating the spindle when it is out of reach. When I am plying, I can quickly retrieve the yarn from one good rotation in the big elbow-nostepinne loops be-

Singles, plies, and cables

fore the spindle begins to go backward and untwist the strands.)

Favorite plying technique #2: Plying sticks

Another means of plying that I like involves what I call *plying sticks*. My plying sticks are an old pair of big, wooden knitting needles. Because the size of the plied skein can be double the size of the singles cops with this method, it is particularly efficient for those who have a larger spindle used primarily for plying or a plying whorl to add to the regular spindle for increased weight.

You ply from two separate cops of singles, instead of from both ends of a single spindle-full. Starting your singles with a brightly colored leader makes this kind of plying much easier to set up because you can immediately locate the inside end of the strand.

1. After filling the handspindle, align the point of a plying stick with the end of the spindle's shaft. Hold these tools together with one hand and carefully slip the cop off the spindle and onto the plying stick. Repeat this process with another cop, slipping it onto a second plying stick. The base of each cop will be at the pointed end of its plying stick and the brightly colored leader will be highly visible.

Transferring yarn from spindle to plying stick

Spinning in the Old Way

How to ply from plying sticks

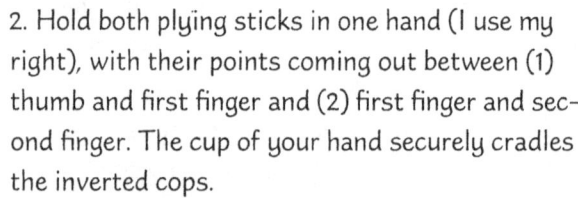

2. Hold both plying sticks in one hand (I use my right), with their points coming out between (1) thumb and first finger and (2) first finger and second finger. The cup of your hand securely cradles the inverted cops.

Draw out the leaders and remove them. Tie the ends of the two singles together with an overhand knot and begin plying, this time drawing the singles from the centers of the two cops.

Spinning three- and four-ply yarns

Three-plies from center-pull balls

For a three-ply yarn, I spin three smaller cops and wind them into individual center-pull balls that I can hold in my hand. Because the quantity of yarn is small, these little center-pull balls do not result in tangling problems the same way that larger center-pull balls do. With one end coming out between each of pair of fingers, I am ready to ply.

Some people like to put the balls in separate bowls and spin from the outsides of the balls. With

Singles, plies, and cables

this set-up, I have difficulty maintaining constant tension on the singles and find that the balls tend to tangle.

Four-plies from both the nostepinne and a plying stick
The simple four-ply yarn involves four single strands spun together at once. For this, we go back to the nostepinne and add in a plying stick.

Slide a cop onto the plying stick (page 153) and draw out the bright leader to locate the end at the center of the cop. Tie together the ends of the inside and outside ends of the strand, and wind the singles onto a nostepinne, following the usual pattern but using the doubled yarn (page 150). Then tie together the doubled strands from the inside and outside of the ball on the nostepinne and spin these together into a four-ply yarn.

If you do not have or prefer not to use a plying stick, you can still use the technique that is my personal favorite for making four-ply yarns. Spin two separate cops and roll each into a ball (these balls do not have to be center-pull). Taking a strand from each ball, wind these yarns together onto the nostepinne. Ply together the doubled strands from the inside and outside of the nostepinne to produce the four-ply yarn.

The first technique results in a four-ply yarn that is one-quarter the length of the singles in a cop and all the ends will come out even. The second technique gives you a four-ply strand that is one-half the length of the singles in a cop, but you

From both the nostepinne and a plying stick

My favorite: two balls of yarn and a nostepinne

may have some leftover singles when you wind the yarns onto the nostepinne.

Cabled yarn

With the skills you are learning, you will be able to spin an infinite number of types of complex yarns. The alternatives are beyond the scope of this book, which focuses on the skills that you will need in order to make your own yarn and be ready to explore the directions of your choice.

Cabling logistics

But before we leave the matter of plying, I need to tell you about the logistics of making what I consider the most exquisite type of multiple-ply yarn: the cabled yarn I described on pages 139 and 140 is made with two two-plies subsequently cabled together to make a finished four-ply that is nothing like the "all at once" four-ply structure.

1. I spin the singles Z, then wind it onto my nostepinne.

2. I now make a two-ply yarn as usual, but ply S with excess twist (that is, I "overply," so the result is not balanced). I wind this two-ply strand onto my nostepinne. The S twist is required in plying because the next step involves doubling the two-ply yarn.

3. I ply both ends of the two-ply strand together using Z twist. The final four-ply yarn should be balanced.

What happens when a strand breaks?

And now I offer you three remedies for a problem that all spinners face when plying: a strand breaks.

Breaks during plying

Singles, plies, and cables

The first solution is to open up the twist at each side of the break, and splice together the two broken ends of yarn. This can be time-consuming and frustrating, because a break usually occurs in a fine, highly twisted section that is difficult to untwist and doesn't give you much fiber to work with when you splice.

Splice

A second solution, simple to achieve, involves overlapping the broken ends by 2 to 3 inches (5 to 7.5 cm) and holding the ends together until they are secured within the plied strand. You need to carefully ensure that the broken ends get caught in the plying twist and don't stick out.

Overlap

Mill production shows me a third option: knotting together the two ends. Lay the loose ends from the knot along the axis of the yarn, going in opposite directions. Hold the ends in place while you insert the plying twist. If you tie your knot carefully, this can make a secure, nearly invisible join.

Knot

ART WASHES AWAY FROM THE SOUL THE DUST OF EVERYDAY LIFE.

Pablo Picasso

> Let us give cheers for that age when again many beautiful unsigned goods are produced. I look forward to the time when again such beautiful goods are used as a matter of course in daily life.
>
> Soetsu Yanagi, *The Unknown Craftsman*

Finishing your yarn
Better than store-bought

When your yarn has been spun, you are not quite done. An unfinished yarn has not achieved its full measure of beauty, and you have not reached the pinnacle of satisfaction with your work.

Skeining yarn

In order to finish your yarn, you first need to make it into a skein. In the oldest skeining method, you wrap the yarn around convenient body parts, such as foot-to-knee or hand-to-elbow. This is fine if you have a strong, flexible body. I do not.

I use the simplest tool possible, a stick with two crosspieces called a *niddy-noddy*. You can expect to experience some consternation when you are first faced with a niddy-noddy, because the crosspieces are at 90-degree angles to one another.

Skeining around body parts

Spinning in the Old Way

Once you become familiar with it, you will love its simplicity and efficiency.

Hold the handspindle by its shaft in one hand, using the position you use for winding on (page 41). Hold the loose end of the yarn and the niddy-noddy's central bar with your other hand.

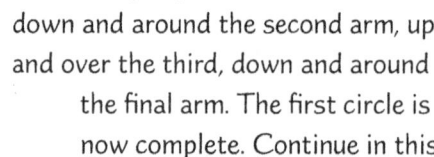
Making a skein with a niddy-noddy

Wind the yarn in a big, continuous circle around the tool's cross-arms: go up and over the first arm, down and around the second arm, up and over the third, down and around the final arm. The first circle is now complete. Continue in this manner, being sure to lay each strand along exactly the same path that you used on the first round, tracing around each arm in the same sequence. Otherwise you will not be able to remove the skein when you are finished.

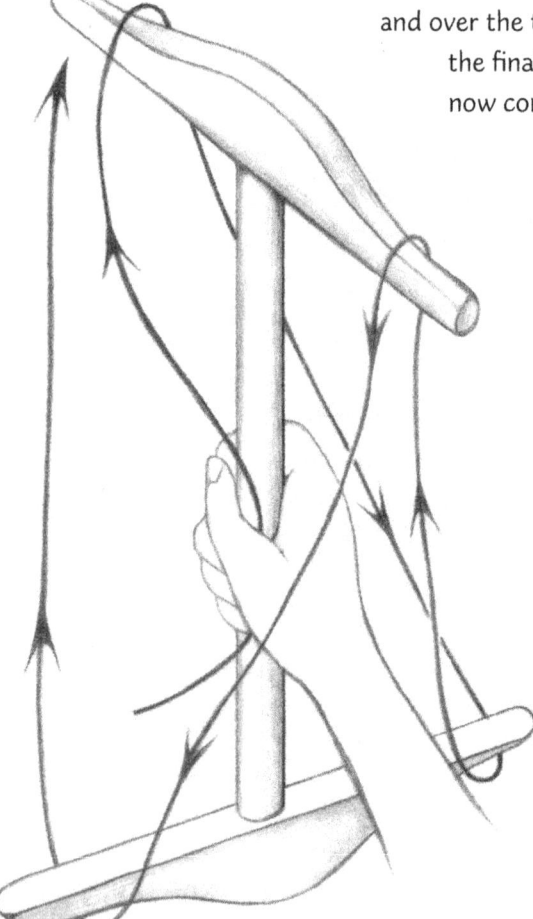

When you have transferred all the yarn from the spindle to the niddy-noddy, tie together the beginning and ending tails.

Finishing your yarn

Before you remove the skein from the niddy-noddy, add two types of skein-ties. These will prevent much hopeless tangling later.

1. First, tie a length of contrasting yarn to the ends. The change in color for this tie will help you quickly find those ends when you need them.

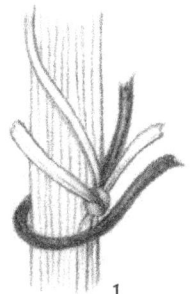

2. Loop that contrasting yarn loosely around all the strands of the skein and tie its ends together with an overhand knot.

3. Next, take three or four other lengths of waste yarn, say 6 to 8 inches (15 to 20 cm) each, and weave them loosely through the skein at evenly spaced intervals. The finer your yarn, the more ties you need. Don't keep the same strands of yarn in each group as you work from tie to tie.

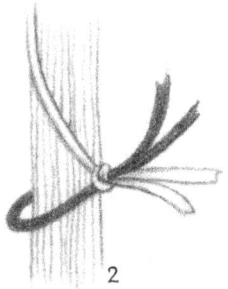

The first skein-tie

The yarn is now ready to slip off one arm of the niddy-noddy, allowing the skein to fall free. On some niddy-noddies, three of the arms have small ridges at their ends to keep the skein from falling

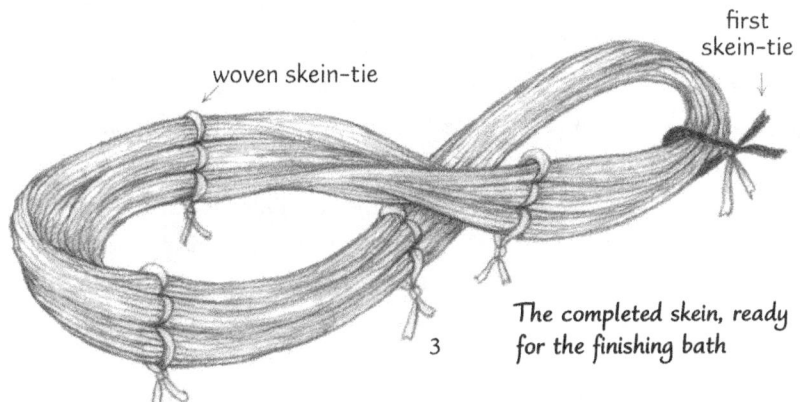

The completed skein, ready for the finishing bath

off before you're ready to take it off. The fourth will be smooth, so you can slip the skein off that one arm and it will be released.

(Note: If you plan to enter your skein in a spinning contest, find out the requirements for judging before you tie your skein. Some contests like the skeins to be more beautiful than practical and require matching skein-ties.)

The water treatment

I have often heard it said that I "boil" my yarn. This is not true. All of my yarn goes through a simmer bath. This step is especially important for singles, because the twist must be neutralized if the end product is to be some form of knitwear.

To finish your yarn, start by preparing a warm bath in a large enameled canner. (The pot must be nonreactive, and the enameled ones are cheaper than stainless steel.) There must be enough water so the yarn can move freely. Add a little liquid dish detergent and place the pot on the stove. Set the yarn on the surface of the water and lightly press it down so it begins to absorb water and starts to sink (the yarn will sink more on its own later, as it absorbs more water).

Warm bath

Gentle simmer

Set the burner at medium to medium high and slowly raise the temperature to a simmer, not a boil (about 160° to 180°F, or roughly 70° to 85°C). Lift and turn the yarn regularly so all the yarn heats evenly. It isn't necessary to lift and turn it constantly. Do not stir the yarn.

Finishing your yarn

For woolen yarns, when the water reaches a simmer turn off the burner and allow the yarn to cool down until the water is comfortable to the hand.

For worsted yarns, once the water reaches a simmer reduce the heat to maintain that temperature for about ten minutes, then turn off the burner and let the water cool in the same way as for woolen yarn.

Why the difference in treatment for woolen and worsted yarns? Woolen yarns are open and lofty. It is easy for the water to penetrate the strands. Worsted yarns are dense, making it more difficult for the water to saturate them. For hybrid yarns that don't fall decidedly into either category, you will need to use your best judgment about how long to simmer the yarn before letting it gradually cool in the water.

After the simmer bath, I thoroughly rinse the skeins in warm water. Be sure to press the yarn down into the water, and squeeze the skein to get the water out. Don't agitate the fiber in hot water or wring out the water unless you are interested in discovering how well it felts!

Cool-down: woolen or worsted

Rinse

A few thoughts about dyeing yarn

When I dye the yarn, I skip the simmer bath and use the dye bath to fulfill the finishing requirement.

Much of my work in the past has been with natural colored wools. My adage was to approach dyeing like death—to stay away from it as long as I could.

Today I find myself doing a lot more dyeing, however, because I want to work with the colors of the traditional Eastern socks, especially those of Central Asia. I use synthetic dyes because I am not particularly knowledgeable about the science of dyeing. To achieve an "old" color palette, I over-dye natural colors. If I want a heathery appearance, I blend colored and white wools before spinning, and dye the completed yarn.

After the dye bath, I thoroughly rinse the skeins, as I do after simmering (page 163). For dyed yarn, I may need to use several rinses before the water stays clear and signals that the rinsing is done.

Spin, snap, and dry

You can hang skeins to drip dry, but if you have a washing machine with a spin-only cycle I strongly recommend using that cycle to hasten the drying. Don't let the water run directly onto the skeins (fill the washer, then add the skeins) and don't let the machine agitate. Just SPIN.

Spin-only cycle

1. When you remove a spun-dry skein from the washer, grab it by one end and pop it like a whip, then grab the other end and repeat the popping. Do this several times to remove the tangles.

Finishing your yarn

2. Then put your hands inside the skein loop and snap them outward vigorously, to straighten all the strands. Work your way around the skein, snapping outward several times, until the skein is tidy and even.

Straightening the finished skein

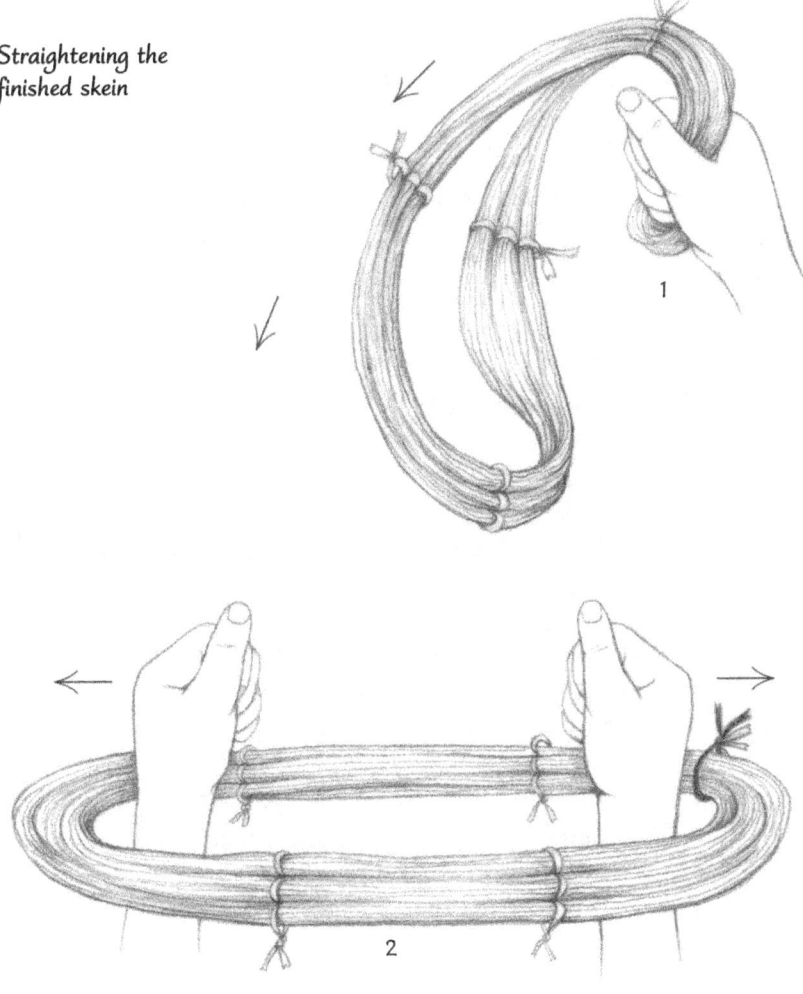

Drying your yarn, and the limited use of blocking

Don't block for knitting

If you plan to knit with your yarn, hang it to dry. Knitting yarns are not blocked by any means—*blocking* refers to drying the yarn under tension. Blocking a knitting yarn will reduce its elasticity and loft. Yes, even my singles yarns hang free.

If you do block a yarn that you later knit with, the first wetting of the finished fabric will relax the yarn and alter the gauge. If you want it to fit properly, you will have to block your knitted piece every time you wash it.

Block for weaving

You should block weaving yarns, especially those destined for use in a warp. Keep the tension light. A simple way to block a skein is to hang it and to place something in the lower loop to weight the skein and hold the strands under slight tension.

Storing skeins

The yarn is now a finished product. To get a skein ready for storage:

1. Grasp the skein, put a thumb in each end of the loop, and rotate your hands to insert twist in the skein as a whole until it feels firm.

2. Fold the skein in its middle so the two sides twist together firmly. Allow the skein to ply back on itself.

Finishing your yarn

3. Tuck one end of the skein into the loop of the other end. The skein is ready to be stored until you need it.

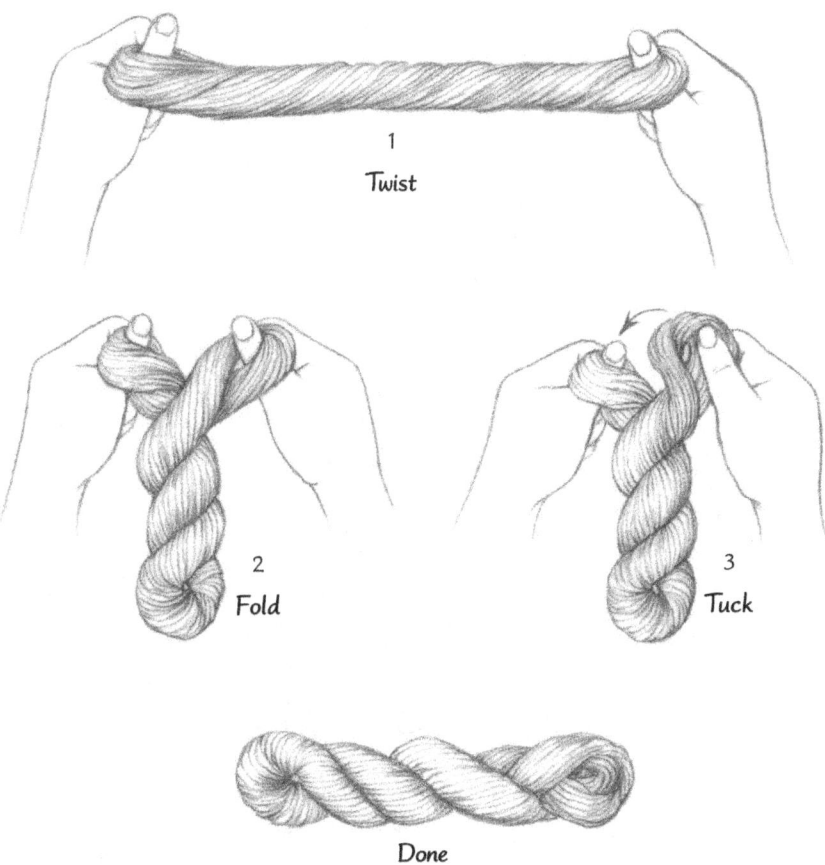

Winding balls

To wind center-pull balls, I drop a skein over a chair back and wind the ball on my nostepinne, described in the information on plying (page 150).

'TIS A GIFT TO BE SIMPLE,
'TIS A GIFT TO BE FREE...

Shaker song

Afterword

I think of myself as a simple person, seeking a less complicated life—not an easy task in today's world.

High-whorling meets my needs, both physically and psychologically. It is a simple, uncluttered task, earthy in all aspects. Perhaps it is this basic quality that I like so well. With this simple tool I can produce yarns for socks that speak of other times, other places. Or I can spin the strands to weave a tapestry rug, ageless in concept and appeal. Both of these primitive art forms mentally free me from a complex, cluttered civilization.

If you are like me, perhaps high-whorling will touch your heart and free your soul.

Selected suppliers

Even if you think you don't know where to start, we still suggest that you assemble your own "begin-to-spin" kit. Choose a high-whorl (or top-whorl) spindle that weighs about 1 ¾ ounces (50 g). Add between 1 and 4 ounces (28.5 and 114 g) of carded Romney roving. You already have the book!

To the best of our knowledge, the following makers and suppliers are active as this book goes to press. Excellent materials and equipment are sometimes produced by very small businesses, many of which run for a long time and some of which vanish. As we prepared this book, one supplier of Akha spindles closed down. As we finished this list, we discovered a new Akha supplier and learned that a source for fibers had changed its focus.

This list is alphabetical by business name or maker's surname.

"General supplier" means that the source carries a range of spindles, fibers, and accessories, including carders, combs, niddy-noddies, and the like. Several of the general suppliers have print catalogs that are include many more items than their web sites suggest. If the web offerings look slim, request a catalog by mail.

When reviewing a general supplier's catalog, use the guidelines in chapter 2 to help you make wise purchases.

I am always finding new delights: keep your eyes open and enjoy the treasure hunt. If you discover, or are the producer of, spindles or fibers that readers of this book should know about, please write me care of the publisher (nomad@nomad-press.com).

Bountiful
Lois and Bud Scarbrough
211 Green Mountain Drive
Livermore, CO 80536
www.bountifulspinweave.com
(970) 482-7746
(877) 586-9332 (orders only)
General supplier.

Carolina Homespun
455 Lisbon Street
San Francisco, CA 94112
www.carolinahomespun.com
(800) 450-7786
(415) 337-6876
General supplier.

Cascade Spindles
Terry Terpening
www.cascadespindles.com
Wooden tools for spinners.
Available through dealers.

Selected suppliers

Gemini Fibres
5062 Mount Albert Road East
Mount Albert, ON L0G 1M0
Canada
www.geminifibres.com
(905) 473-1033
(800) 564-9665
  General supplier. Spindles by Tom Forrester; Akha spindles; plying nostepinnes, breed-specific wools.

Golding Precision Fiber Tools
Tom and Diane Golding
Meadowsweet Farm
849 Saxtons River Road
Saxtons River, VT 05154
www.dropspindle.info
(800) 710-1872
  Simple to intricate spindles with bronze alloy ring on whorl. Spindle stands for plying from their spindles (two- and three-ply models).

Greensleeves Spindles
Elizabeth and Bart Dailey
4505 N. Canyon Road
Provo, UT 84604
www.greensleevesspindles.com
(802) 226-7582
  Medieval-themed spindles, spindle stand for plying (up to four spindles), and short-run custom rovings.

Halcyon Yarn
12 Bath Street
Bath, ME 04530
www.halcyonyarn.com
(800) 341-0282
  General supplier. Some breed-specific wools.

Journey Wheel
Jonathan and Sheila Bosworth
29 Main Street
Acton, MA 01720
www.journeywheel.com

(978) 264-0584
  Spindles in many woods, as well as unusual materials.

Magpie Wood Works
John Jenkins
316 Parkwood Drive
Grand Junction, CO 81503
(970) 256-1257
  Spindles. Carried by retailers.

Mielke's Fiber Arts
2550 Co. Rd. II
Rudolph, WI 54475-9409
www.mielkesfiberarts.com
(715) 435-4494
  General supplier. Includes spindles from Adam's Woodshop and some breed-specific wools.

Misty Mountain Farm
www.mistymountainfarm.com
(540) 937-4707

Quick-start spindles

You'll want a *real* spindle. But before you have one, you can experiment with a make-at-home model. David Reed Smith offers free plans for a Lisard Ultralight, made from a bamboo skewer, posterboard (or cereal box), and a paperclip (www.davidreedsmith.com). Melissa Croci's design for a spindle made with discarded CDs and hardware-store materials is available as a free PDF download (published in *Spin-Off* Spring 1999; available at www.interweave.com/spin/projects/cdspindles.pdf). Both will let you play with twist.

Breed-specific fibers in top and/or roving form, including wools and wool blends: their own Finn, Lincoln, and Finn-Lincoln crosses; also Coopworth, Corriedale, and others.

Paradise Fibers
W, 919 Paradise Road
Spokane, WA 99224
www.paradisefibers.com
(509) 456-4345
   General supplier. Breed-specific fibers.

David Reed Smith
www.davidreedsmith.com
   A continually evolving line of handspindles, a number of which have been high-whorl models. Available from The Wool Room.

Spinner's Choice
974 N. Highway 99W
P.O. Box 191
Dundee, OR 97115
www.spinnerschoice.com
(503) 538-4741
   Spindles in a variety of woods.

Susan's Fiber Shop
Susan McFarland
N 250 Highway A
Columbus, WI 53925
www.susansfibershop.com

(920) 623-4237
(920) 623 0120 fax
   General supplier.

The Vermont Spindle Company
Bill Mutschler
43 Maple Lane
East Burke, VT 05832
www.coppermoose.com
www.spinningfiber.com
(802) 626-6002
(866) 443-4237 for orders
   Spindles and breed-specific fibers. Spindles also available through dealers.

Woodland Woolworks
P.O. Box 850
Carlton, OR 97111
www.woodlandwoolworks.com
(800) 547-3725 for orders
   General supplier.

Woodchuck Products
Rod Stevens
23 Vista del Ocaso
Taos, NM 87557
woodchuckproduct@netscape.com
(717) 586–6162 or maybe 505 737-9608
   Spindles, nostepinnes, niddy-noddies, and other useful and beautiful items.

The Woolery
PO Box 468
Murfreesboro, NC 27855
www.woolery.com
(800) 441-9665
(252) 398-4581
(252) 398-5974 fax
   General supplier.

Woolly Designs
Tracy and Jean Eichheim
2111 Black Canyon Road
Crawford, CO 81415-9554
www.woollydesigns.com
(970) 921-3834
   Spindles and homegrown fleece.

The Wool Room
Southeast, NY 10509
(845) 279- 7624
(845) 278-5947 fax
www.woolroom.com
   Well-selected tools and fibers, often from very small suppliers.

Suggested reading

Buchanan, Rita. "Mastering Twist." *Spin-Off* 21, no. 4 (Winter 1997): 34–44.

Buchanan, Rita, and Deborah Robson. "Introduction to Spinning." *Spin-Off* brochure. Loveland, Colorado: Interweave Press, 1995.

———. "Low Tech, High Satisfaction." *Spin-Off* brochure. Loveland, Colorado: Interweave Press, 1995.

Crowfoot, Grace M. *Methods of Handspinning in Egypt and the Sudan.* Bankfield Museum Notes, ser. 2, no. 12. Halifax, England: County Borough of Halifax, 1931.

Davenport, Elsie G. *Your Handspinning.* Pacific Grove, California: Select Books, 1964.

Gibson-Roberts, Priscilla A. "Handspun Yarns for Ethnic Socks." *Knitter's* no. 36 (Fall 1994): 88–91.

———. "Summer Spinning, A Return to the Hand Spindle." *Knitter's* no. 35 (Summer 1994): 56–59.

———. *Ethnic Socks and Stockings.* Sioux Falls, South Dakota: XRX, 1995.

———. "The High-whorl Spindle." *Spin-Off* 19, no. 1 (Spring 1995): 60–65.

———. *Knitting in the Old Way.* Loveland, Colorado: Interweave Press, 1985. See also the expanded edition of this book below (2004).

———. *Cowichan Indian Sweaters: A Pacific Northwest Tradition.* Saint Paul, Minnesota: Dos Tejedoras Fiber Arts, 1989.

Gibson-Roberts, Priscilla A., and Deborah Robson. *Knitting in the Old Way: Designs and Techniques from Ethnic Sweaters.* Fort Collins, Colorado: Nomad Press, 2004.

Hochberg, Bette. *Handspindles.* Santa Cruz, California: Bette and Bernard Hochberg, 1979.

———. *Spin, Span, Spun: Fact and Folklore for Spinners.* Santa Cruz, California: Bette and Bernard Hochberg, 1977.

Mason, Lynn DeRose. "A Spindle Miscellany: Akha Spinning." *Spin-Off* 19, no. 1 (Spring 1995): 86.

Raven, Lee. *Hands On Spinning.* Loveland, Colorado: Interweave Press, 1987.

Yanagi, Soetsu (Muneyoshi). *The Unknown Craftsman.* Rev. ed. New York and Tokyo: Kodansha America and Kodansha International, 1989.

Index

active-twist yarns, 131—132
adding fiber, *see* joining fiber
Africa, high-whorl spindles, 23
Akha spindles, 126—127
alpaca, 64
angora, 68
angular draw, 111
animal fibers, 64—69
Asia
   Akha spindles, 126—127
   community plying, 146
   Eastern socks, 13, 147, 164
   high-whorl spindles, 14, 21, 23
   Karakul fleece, 68

balanced yarns
   appearance of, 93, 130, 131
   cabled yarns, 140
   checking twist, 138—139
   knitting with, 132
   making, 129, 130—131, 137—138
balls, center-pull, *see* center-pull balls
batts
   carding, 77
   converting to rovings, 84—85
   definition, 82
beehive cops, 107—108
bird's nests, making, 82, 83
blocking, 166
braid wools, 66
broken yarns, fixing, 124, 156—157
bulky yarns
   recommended spindle weights, 48, 49
   Salish spindles, use of, 124
   supported spinning for, 91—92
   twist and diameter, 134, 135
   wool choices, 135

cabled yarns, 139—140, 156
carding, 70—71, 73—78

cashmere, 64
catching yarn, *see* securing yarn on the spindle
center-pull balls
   plying from, 147—148, 154—155
   winding from skeins, 167
Central Asia, *see* Asia
Churro, 68
cleaning fiber, 73, 78
clockwise spindle rotation, 31, 92—93
Columbia, 66, 67
combing, 71—72, 78—82
community plying, 146—147
conditioning fiber, 84—87
cone-shaped cops, 109
cops
   definition, 55
   ways of building, 106—109
Cormo, 65
Corriedale, 66, 67
cotton, 64, 69
counterclockwise spindle rotation, 31, 92—93
Cowichan sweaters, 13, 124, 133
crimp, 65, 134
crossbred wools, 67
cup hooks, 51—52

diameter
   maintaining consistency of, 120—122
   measuring, 47, 118
distaffs, 87
diz, 82
DK yarns, 48, 49
double-whorl spindles, 53, 54—55
down-shaft whorls, 52, 53
drafting
   drafting zone, 105
   overview, 36—37, 39—40
   pre-drafting, 104
   woolen drafting, 112, 113—114
   worsted drafting, 112, 114—117

draw methods
   angular draw, 111
   horizontal draw, 110—111
   long draw, 112, 113—114
   short draw, 112, 114—117
   vertical draw, 109—110
   worsted draw from the fold, 116—117
   see also drafting
drop spindles, *see* suspended spinning
drum-carded fibers, 74
dual-coated wools, 67—68
dyeing, 163—164

Eastern sock traditions, 13—14, 147, 164
Eastern spinning, 106, 107, 110
Egypt, high-whorl spindles, 23
elongated hooks, 50
ethnic traditions
   Akha spindles, 126—127
   community plying, 146—147
   Cowichan sweaters, 13, 124, 133
   overhead rings for plying, 143
   Peruvian hand-wrap plying, 143—146
   Salish Indian spindles, 124—126
   socks, 13—14, 133, 147, 164
   use of singles yarns, 133—134
Europe
   high-whorl spindles, 14, 23
   low-whorl spindles, 21
   overhead plying rings, 143
   sock traditions, 13, 133—134

fiber
   attaching a new supply, 41, 123
   conditioning, 84—87
   positioning for spinning, 87—89

Index

storing, 82–84
types of, 64–69
fiber preparation
  combing, 78–82
  hand carding, 73–78
  woolen versus worsted, 70–72
fine wools, 65–66, 134, 135
fine yarns
  Akha spindles, use of, 126–127
  fiber choices, 65
  skein ties for, 161
  spindle weights for, 48, 49
fingering weight yarns, 48, 49
finishing
  drying, 166
  removing excess water, 164–165
  samples, 122
  skeining yarn, 159–162
  water treatment, 162–163
Finn, 66, 67
flax, 23, 64
fold, worsted draw from, 116–117
four-ply yarns, 137, 155–156

half-hitch yarn attachment, 26–27
hand alignment, 106
hand carding, 70–71, 73–78
handspindles, *see* spindles
hand-wrap plying, 143–146
heavyweight yarns
  spindle weights for, 48, 49
  twist and diameter, 134, 135
hemp, 64
high-peaked hooks, 50–51
high-whorl spindles
  anatomy, 22
  benefits of using, 16–18
  comparison to low-whorl spindles, 24–27
  historical perspective, 14, 21, 23
  selecting, 45–46
hook types, 50–52
  see also securing yarn on the spindle
horizontal draw, 110–111

joining fiber

attaching a new fiber supply, 41, 123
attaching to leader yarn, 99
fixing breaks, 124, 156–157

Karakul, 67, 68
Karashire, 67
kid mohair, 64, 68
knitting
  active twist in, 132
  with singles yarns, 136
knitting-worsted yarns, 48, 49, 65

laceweight yarns, 48, 49
lap spindles, *see* supported spinning
leader yarn
  attaching, 32–33, 98–99
  beginning without, 99–101
lightweight yarns, 48, 49
Lincoln, 67
long draw, 112, 113–114
long wools/fibers, 64, 66, 134, 135
low-whorl spindles, 21, 24–27

medium wools, 66, 67, 134, 135
medium-weight yarns, 48, 49, 134, 135
Merino, 65
Middle East
  community plying, 146
  high-whorl spindles, 14, 21
  Karakul fleece, 68
  sock traditions, 13
mohair, 64, 68

Navajo-Churro, 68
neutral hand position, 106
niddy-noddies
  how to use, 159–160
  types of, 60–61
nostepinnes
  plying from, 147–148, 151–153, 155–156
  types of, 60, 61
  winding yarn onto, 150–151
notches on whorls, 55–58

Peruvian hand-wrap plying, 143–146

plying
  active twist, 131–132
  balanced twist, 130–132, 137–139
  basic principles, 48, 129, 136–137, 141
  broken yarn, 156–157
  cabled yarns, 139–140, 156
  community plying, 146–147
  four-ply yarns, 137, 155–156
  off the nostepinne, 147–153, 155–156
  overhead rings, use of, 143
  Peruvian hand-wrap plying, 143–146
  plying sticks, 61, 153–154
  stands or bowls, use of, 142–143
  three-ply yarns, 137, 154–155
  two-ply yarns, 48, 49, 136–137, 151–154

Rambouillet, 65
rejoining fiber, *see* joining fiber
relaxed twist, 131–132
removable whorls, 54
rolags, 77, 83
rolling the spindle, 94–97
Romney, 66, 67
rotation of spindles
  beginning to twist, 34
  directions of, 31, 36, 92–93
  seated versus standing, 94–97
roving
  carding, 77
  conditioning for spinning, 86–87
  spinning with, 38–39
  storing, 83

S-twist yarns
  active twist, 131, 132
  gauging twist, 119
  seated versus standing position, 94–97
  spindle rotation and, 31, 92–93
Salish Indian spindles, 124–126
sample cards, 121–122
scouring, 73, 78

175

seated spinning, 42, 94, 95, 96
  see also supported spinning
securing yarn on the spindle
  attaching starter or leader yarn, 32–33, 98–99
  catching yarn at the spindle top, 32–33, 102, 103–104
  setting the twist, 134, 162–163
shafts, spindle, 58–59
Shetland yarns, 48, 49
short draw, 112, 114–117
short fibers, 64, 65–66
singles yarns, 132–136
skeins
  assessing twist in, 131
  preparing for storage, 166–167
  skein-ties, 161–162
  using a niddy-noddy, 159–160
socks, Eastern and Western traditions, 13–14, 133, 147, 164
Spelsau, 68
spin-cycle, use of, 164–165
spindles
  defined, 9–10
  high-whorl versus low-whorl, 24–27
  hooks, 50–52
  selecting, 45–46, 48–49
  shafts, 58–59
  types of, 21
  weights of, 29, 45, 48, 49
  whorls, 52–58
  see also high-whorl spindles
spinning, definition, 9
splicing yarn, 157
  see also joining fiber
sportweight yarns, 48, 49
standing while spinning, 94, 95
  see also suspended spinning
starter yarn, attaching, 32–33
  see also leader yarn
stockinette stitch
  active twist in, 132
  with singles yarns, 136
storage

fiber, 82–84
skeins, 166–167
supplies
  recommendations, 29–30
  tools, 59–61
supported spinning
  definition, 31, 91
  techniques, 42, 95
  twist directions, 94, 96
  yarn characteristics, 91–92, 112
suspended spinning
  definition, 31, 91
  draw methods, 109–111
  techniques, 34, 95
  twist directions, 94, 95, 96
  yarn characteristics, 92, 112
swan's-neck hooks, 50–51

threading the hook, 32–33
three-ply yarns, 137, 154–155
tools, 59–61
top, 83
traditional methods, *see* ethnic traditions
twist
  balanced twist, 93, 130, 131, 132
  checking, 138–139
  controlling, 40
  definition, 130
  directions of, 31, 92–93
  maintaining consistency of, 120–122
  measuring, 118–119
  in plied yarns, 137–139
  setting, 134, 162–163
  in singles yarns, 134–136
two-ply yarns
  balanced twist, 137–139
  characteristics, 136–137
  plying methods, 151–154
  wraps per inch, 48, 49

underplied yarns, 139

vertical draw, 109–110
volume gauge, 82

washing fiber, 73, 78
water treatment for setting twist, 162–163
weights, of spindles, 29, 45, 48, 49

Western sock traditions, 13–14
Western spinning, 106
whorls
  notches on, 55–58
  position of, 24, 52–54
  removable, 54
winding yarn
  building the cop, 106–109
  off the spindle, 148–151
  onto the spindle, 35, 41, 101–102
woolen yarns
  characteristics, 70–71, 112
  fiber preparation, 70–71
  spinning methods, 112, 113–114
wools, types of, 65–68
worsted yarns
  characteristics, 71–72, 112
  fiber preparation, 71–72
  spinning methods, 112, 114–117
wraps per inch
  measuring, 46–47
  singles yarns, 134, 135
  two-ply yarns, 48, 49

yarn gauges, 46
yarns
  maintaining consistency of, 120–122
  size descriptions, 46–47, 48, 49
  see also specific weights and plies

Z-twist yarns
  active twist, 131, 132
  gauging twist, 119
  in knitting, 132, 136
  seated versus standing position, 94–97
  spindle rotation and, 31, 92–93

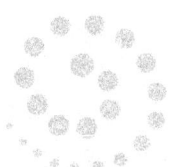

www.ingramcontent.com/pod-product-compliance
Lightning Source LLC
Chambersburg PA
CBHW031630160426

43196CB00006B/358